Spiritual Warfare

How to Protect Yourself and Your Loved Ones from Spiritual Attacks, Energy Vampires, Entities, Demons, and Curses

© Copyright 2025 - All rights reserved.

The content contained within this book may not be reproduced, duplicated, or transmitted without direct written permission from the author or the publisher.

Under no circumstances will any blame or legal responsibility be held against the publisher, or author, for any damages, reparation, or monetary loss due to the information contained within this book, either directly or indirectly.

Legal Notice:

This book is copyright protected. It is only for personal use. You cannot amend, distribute, sell, use, quote, or paraphrase any part, or the content within this book, without the consent of the author or publisher.

Disclaimer Notice:

Please note the information contained within this document is for educational and entertainment purposes only. All effort has been executed to present accurate, up-to-date, reliable, and complete information. No warranties of any kind are declared or implied. Readers acknowledge that the author is not engaging in the rendering of legal, financial, medical, or professional advice. The content within this book has been derived from various sources. Please consult a licensed professional before attempting any techniques outlined in this book.

By reading this document, the reader agrees that under no circumstances is the author responsible for any losses, direct or indirect, that are incurred as a result of the use of the information contained within this document, including, but not limited to, errors, omissions, or inaccuracies.

Your Free Gift
(only available for a limited time)

Thanks for getting this book! If you want to learn more about various spirituality topics, then join Mari Silva's community and get a free guided meditation MP3 for awakening your third eye. This guided meditation mp3 is designed to open and strengthen ones third eye so you can experience a higher state of consciousness. Simply visit the link below the image to get started.

https://spiritualityspot.com/meditation
Or, Scan the QR code!

Table of Contents

INTRODUCTION 1
CHAPTER 1: UNDERSTANDING THE BATTLES..3
CHAPTER 2: THE ARMOR OF GOD AS SPIRITUAL DEFENSE 16
CHAPTER 3: RECOGNIZING THE ENEMY'S TACTICS 29
CHAPTER 4: THE POWER OF PRAYER AND FASTING 42
CHAPTER 5: SPIRITUAL DEFENSE: STANDING FIRM AGAINST DARKNESS..54
CHAPTER 6: OVERCOMING CURSES AND GENERATIONAL BONDAGE 67
CHAPTER 7: PROTECTING THE FAMILY THROUGH FAITH 79
CHAPTER 8: TESTING THE SOURCE OF SPIRITUAL INFLUENCES..90
CHAPTER 9: LIVING VICTORIOUSLY IN CHRIST................................100
CONCLUSION 111
HERE'S ANOTHER BOOK BY MARI SILVA THAT YOU MIGHT LIKE 114
YOUR FREE GIFT (ONLY AVAILABLE FOR A LIMITED TIME) 115
REFERENCES..116
IMAGE SOURCES 120

Introduction

Sun Tzu, a strategist, philosopher, and one-time Chinese general, rightly said: *"Know thy enemy and know yourself; in a hundred battles, you will never be defeated."*

This book on Spiritual warfare gives you a hands-on approach to dealing with spiritual challenges. Unlike many books on spiritual warfare and influences, it captures a comprehensive, practical, and Bible-based strategy for dealing with the Devil's tactics. It tackles lesser-known evils, like curses, entities, and energy vampires. Against feeding you with vague theologies and fear-based prophecies, this book empowers you with practical and relevant tools to identify, resist, and overcome spiritual oppression in all its forms.

It'll deepen your spiritual understanding and strengthen your faith in spiritual challenges, equipping you to recognize and overcome spiritual attacks in their many forms – protecting you and your loved ones. You were designed by Christ to live in freedom.

This book on spiritual warfare shows you how to live your best life as one who has received victory by helping you:

- Grasp the meaning and background of spiritual warfare
- Recognize the enemy's tactics and spiritual attacks
- Uncover the power of prayer and fasting
- Understand how to use the armor to protect yourself and your loved ones
- Test spiritual influences to avoid deception

- Discover Biblical and spiritual tools to break curses and resist entities
- Build a solid defense against demonic oppression using faith, prayer, and discernment

Spiritual battles are real and ongoing between the forces of good and evil, with you at the center, whether you choose to see it or not. Therefore, it's pivotal to learn how to spot enemies a mile away by understanding how they think and act – *and shielding yourself from their attacks.*

If you've always wanted a book on Spiritual Warfare or are in one but don't know where to begin or how to deal with it, consider this book your warfare manual. Your battles with spiritual forces become straightforward and exciting with this book. You'll never be surprised by the enemy's attacks because you'll be acquainted with His patterns and flow with the victory in Christ Jesus.

Chapter 1: Understanding the Battles

"For we wrestle not against flesh and blood, but against principalities, against powers, against the rulers of the darkness of this world, against spiritual wickedness in high places." - Ephesians 6:12

War is constantly mentioned in news outlets, articles, social media, and books. It's a key part of human civilization, and no developed nation today doesn't have an account - a history - of contention, battle for freedom, or warfare.

It's a given that you or someone you know has survived or experienced war in one way or another. This explains only one thing: you're in a constant battle in the physical world against territorial disputes, control over resources, for higher power and authority, for freedom, and sometimes for peace. These are a constant in the physical world. So, how much more in the spiritual world?

The battles of the mind and faith are often the hardest to overcome.[1]

Ephesians 6.12 describes that people should be more conscious of the unseen than the seen. Ephesus was a large city, an epicenter for worshipping many Roman and Greek gods. Although Paul had converted many to Christianity in Ephesus and its surroundings, years passed, and he saw the need to remind and encourage the Ephesian Christians where the true contention for their soul was.

Paul was writing to believers who were not physically imprisoned, as he was then (60-64 C.E. under the Romans), but may have been victims of spiritual imprisonment. The context of this ideology doesn't sound sane, but Paul, who, among the apostles commissioned by Jesus, undoubtedly understood how the spirit realm operates and had fought and won many spiritual battles. Paul writes that the contention for your soul, your life, is not mainly flesh and blood. This means it isn't physical. Can you imagine that, as believers, your enemies don't attack head-on physically? Every attack may be manifested physically because that is where you would feel the impact the most, but they are not physically originated. These attacks are spearheaded by spiritual entities – First, territorial spirits (principalities), then dark powers, then the world's rulers of darkness, and above all, spiritual wickedness in high places.

It's enough that you must contend against the constant wickedness in the hearts of men due to sin's nature that every man is naturally born into. Yet, Paul writes that this isn't the only thing to be worried about.

There are dark and powerful forces that cannot be seen unless revealed by God, and as believers, you're constantly in a war with these forces. You may think, "So, unbelievers don't get to face these forces?"

In fact, since being in your mother's womb, war has been waged against you from the kingdom of darkness. "Why?" This is discussed in the origin of spiritual warfare. The origin of your spiritual warfare springs from the creation of Adam and Eve in the Garden of Eden. However, what matters more is what the second Adam (Jesus Christ) did, which is revealed in the scriptures:

"For since by man came death, by man came also the resurrection of the dead. For as in Adam all die, even so in Christ shall all be made alive." - 1 Corinthians 15:21-22.

"Wherefore, as by one man sin entered into the world, and death by sin; and so death passed upon all men, for that all have sinned: (for until the law sin was in the world: but sin is not imputed when there is no law. Nevertheless, death reigned from Adam to Moses, even over them that had not sinned after the similitude of Adam's transgression, who is the figure of him that was to come. But not as an offense, so also is the free gift. For if through the offense of one many be dead, much more the grace of God, and the gift by grace, which is by one man, Jesus Christ, hath abounded unto many." - Romans 5:12-15.

The Origin of Spiritual Warfare

Where did it all begin? Did the war waged by the kingdom of darkness against the children of God start when we surrendered our lives to Christ? Definitely not. The moment you were in your mother's womb, war was waged against you. What, then, separates a Christian from every person on Earth? It's the new identity - the identity of Christ who conquered death and overthrew the grave forever. This is the life that now flows in you, the life of the One who fought and defeated the enemy. This life produces hope.

You may ask, "If Jesus Christ has defeated the enemy, why do I still need to fight? Why is war still being waged against me as a Christian?" Even though Christ defeated the enemy, You must constantly uphold this victory and remind the enemy of His position in you. The world you live in is a fallen world, and the enemy is the god of this world. He is not tired and weary of resisting God's Kingdom and all that God stands for on Earth. Here's what Peter says after the resurrection of Christ:

"Be sober, be vigilant; because your adversary the Devil, as a roaring lion, walketh about, seeking whom he may devour" - 1 Peter 5:8 KJV.

However, the defeated Devil still deceives and attacks people. So, who is the enemy, and why does he despise the seed of man?

A Rebellion in Heaven

Satan, known as Lucifer (meaning "morning star"), was once an anointed Cherub and the leader of Heaven's choir. Before his rebellion, which led to his fall, he was perfect in beauty and extravagantly in excellence for worship towards God. Yet he sinned in his heart when, in pride, he lifted himself above and against God's authority. Ezekiel describes this in chapter 28:

> *"... 'You were the seal of perfection, full of wisdom and perfect in beauty. You were in Eden, the garden of God; every precious stone adorned you: carnelian, chrysolite and emerald, topaz, onyx and jasper, lapis lazuli, turquoise and beryl. Your settings and mountings were made of gold; on the day you were created, they were prepared. You were anointed as a guardian cherub, for so I ordained you. You were on the holy mount of God; you walked among the fiery stones. You were blameless in your ways from the day you were created till wickedness was found in you... Your heart became proud on account of your beauty, and you corrupted your wisdom because of your splendor. So, I threw you to the earth; I made a spectacle of you before kings."* -Ezekiel 28:12-15, 17 NIV.

Lucifer was perfect, but due to the thoughts of his heart, he fell into imperfection. What were the thoughts of his heart? According to the prophet Isaiah, Lucifer exalted himself above God and everything that represented God.

> *"How art thou fallen from heaven, O Lucifer, son of the morning! How art thou cut down to the ground, which didst weaken the nations! For thou hast said in thine heart, I will ascend into heaven, I will exalt my throne above the stars of God: I will sit also upon the mount of the congregation, in the sides of the north: I will ascend above the heights of the clouds; I will be like the most High. Yet thou shalt be brought down to hell, to the sides of the pit."* -Isaiah 14:12-15 KJV.

Lucifer's five "wills" are broken down as follows:

"I will ascend into Heaven." – According to the scriptures, there are three heavens. The Earth and its atmosphere (cosmic heaven), the Spiritual Heaven (according to Daniel 10:12-14), and the Heaven described by Paul in 2 Corinthians 12:1-4, where the throne of God resides, the highest Heaven.

"I will exalt my throne above the stars of God." – "Stars of God" signifies God's Heavenly angels (Revelation 12:3-4, 22:16). Lucifer wanted dominion over all God's angels.

"I will sit also upon the mount of the congregation, in the sides of the north." – The mount of the congregation can be interpreted as a seat of God's supremacy as Judge. Lucifer desired to be the ruler over all creation.

"I will ascend above the heights of the clouds." – Clouds represent the glory and presence of God (Exodus 40:34-35). Lucifer desired to ascend above God's glory and presence and establish his own presence.

"I will be like the Most High." – Lucifer didn't say he wanted to surpass the Most High. He knew that was impossible. He desired to become like the Most High. Representing complete independence from the power, authority, and dominion of God.

Lucifer rebelled against God with these thoughts. The most obscured part is that he convinced a third of Heaven's angels to buy into his deceit. If Lucifer could convince angels who witnessed the glory of God to betray Him, then he believed he had a better chance with men.

After the rebellion, a war broke out in Heaven. Michael led an army of Heaven's angels against the Devil and his angels, defeating and banishing them into the abyss for good (Revelation 12:7-9). How does this affect you? The answer is *"Jealousy."* It isn't a coincidence that man was created where the Devil and his angels fell after Heaven's war. Not that Man's creation mattered greatly to him, but the purpose of man's creation was indeed unique.

Man represented everything the Devil fought and betrayed God for. The dominion the Devil sought was granted as a bonus pack to man – "Be fruitful," "Have dominion." Man was created for God's pleasure, as was Lucifer before he fell. The difference was that man is a limited edition formed by God, using God's genetic code carrying God's breath (life). You were created in His image and His likeness. Have you ever heard the saying, "Like father, like son?"

Lucifer rebelled against God.[2]

This was enough to drive the Devil mad, and because he knew he couldn't touch God, he sought to touch the heart of God, which was Mankind. He convinced Eve to desire what he desired, and you know how the story ends. However, he wanted what man had – authority and dominion. When Adam fell, he automatically relinquished his authority and dominion on Earth to his new master (the Devil), whom he chose to obey instead of God. However, the Bible reveals that the Devil was again punished for deceiving man:

> *"And the LORD God said unto the serpent, because thou hast done this, thou art cursed above all cattle, and above every beast of the field; upon thy belly shalt thou go, and dust shalt thou eat all the days of thy life: and I will put enmity between thee and the woman, and between thy seed and her seed; it shall bruise thy head, and thou shalt bruise his heel."* - Genesis 3:14-15 KJV.

This curse is why the Devil is in constant war with us. The Devil will forever be an enemy of whoever is born of a man and a greater enemy of whoever is born of God. Being born of God is a triumph over the Devil. It means he is being defeated for a third time. This victory comes in the name and authority of Jesus, a gift to everyone born of God.

Physical Signs You're Experiencing Spiritual Warfare

The Devil has brought the fight to man before you could tell wrong from right. He is not to be taken lightly. He is clever, witty, and much older than you. However, it doesn't bring his strength and wisdom anywhere near God's. He fell because he chose to go against the will of God. He chose the wrong path, which led to eternal punishment. He knew he could never go back because of his corrupted heart. Hence, he chose war.

He also chose to deceive you and make you feel like you don't have a choice over bondage or his oppression. This is not the truth. Whatever is inconsistent with God's word is false and should be immediately dealt with. Remember, he was a serpent in the Garden of Eden, which makes him subtle and devious.

You must know the Devil's many attributes, personality, and portfolio to know how he attacks. You know he is the accuser, the deceiver, and a proud being, but God also calls him a murderer and a liar - father of all liars - (John 8:44). He is called a thief, a killer of anything that has life, a destroyer (John 10:10), a devouring predator, and the tempter.

> "Then was Jesus led up of the Spirit into the wilderness to be tempted of the Devil.... And when the tempter came to him, he said, If thou be the Son of God, command that these stones be made bread." - Matthew 4:1, 3 KJV

Now you know who the Devil is, a few of his schemes of attack are:

Fear

> "For God hath not given us the spirit of fear; but of power, and of love, and of a sound mind." - 2 Timothy 1:7 KJV

God says that fear is a spirit, and He didn't give that spirit to you. If the spirit of fear is not of God, it means it was given by the Devil. Why would the Devil provide you with something you didn't order? The Devil is clever and devious. You didn't need to order fear directly to have it. The Devil stages situations and circumstances around you with a bonus package of fear. The seed of fear gets into you by engaging in those activities. It stays there without you noticing, growing, germinating until, one day, you feel a wave of emotion you're pretty sure wasn't there before (if you can discern).

You see a post or a picture, hear the news, and imagine it could be you or someone close to you. This fear that went unnoticed was an arrow from the enemy camp. It goes through the gates of your eyes and ears, and your heart nurtures it long enough to play in your thoughts like a movie. If you do not rebuke it immediately in the name of Jesus, it stays.

"Submit yourselves therefore to God. Resist the Devil, and he will flee from you." -James 4:7 KJV.

In some cases, you only have to confess the fear to activate it, such as death, despair, anxiety, depression, anguish, loneliness, etc. You say what you're afraid of (a lie from hell), and it becomes reality. Confession not aligned with God's Word is a lie and should be disbanded. If you feel a negative emotion, you should immediately confess God's Word and rebuke the emotion.

"Whoso offereth praise glorifieth me: and to him that ordereth his conversation aright will I shew the salvation of God." – Psalm 50:23 KJV

"A man's belly shall be satisfied with the fruit of his mouth; and with the increase of his lips shall he be filled. Death and life are in the power of the tongue: and they that love it shall eat the fruit thereof." – Proverbs 18:20-21

Despair

In 2 Corinthians 11:23-30, Paul lists his persecutions. He suffered for the gospel's cause and was imprisoned for preaching the good news. It was debilitating and demoralizing, and if you were in the same situation, you may have soon conceded, yet Paul remained firm in his trust in God.

This is the Gospel, and Jesus assures us in Matthew 5 that we are blessed when we go through these for His sake. The Devil hates the good news, which is salvation to those who believe and confess (Romans 10:9). He aims to depopulate the Kingdom of Heaven by sending life issues your way and causing despair to make your soul weary to the point of breakdown. However, God's grace is sufficient for you. His strength is made perfect in your weakness (2 Corinthians 12:9).

Weariness

You sometimes feel weariness in your body and give it names like stress, fatigue, tiredness, or anxiety. However, it can get deeper. Through the Bible, you see instances where Jesus reassures us of "rest"' when we come to Him in a wearied state. If Jesus is reassuring you of rest, it's not only physical rest. If it isn't entirely physical, it means weariness is not wholly a physical state of tiredness. It can mean that you experience fatigue, exhaustion, and frustration in your soul and spirit.

This is the Devil's scheme to put you in a position of unwieldiness, causing delays and constant toiling without results, leading to frustration, emotional exhaustion, and breakdown. A good example is the hardship of God's people, Israel, under their oppressor, the Egyptians. When they got to a breaking point and couldn't take it anymore, the Bible says, "*in their slavery, they cried out...and God heard their groaning*" (Exodus 2:23-25).

"*Blessed are the poor in spirit, for theirs is the Kingdom of Heaven.*" – Matthew 5:3

Other examples of the Devil's scheme are:
- Weakness
- Procrastination
- Doubt
- Failure
- Loss
- Anguish
- Sickness and Infirmities
- Death

Biblical Examples of Spiritual Warfare and How the Patriarchs Overcame Them

The Bible is complete. It dissects and diagnoses every issue you may ever encounter. However, it doesn't end there. It offers prescriptions and necessary tools to tackle each issue. The word *"offer"* is used because you always have the choice to follow God's methods. Biblical characters, "Divine Patriarchs," were pivotal in helping us understand God's ways, His personality, and how He deals with every matter. God is purposeful. He's a master strategist in warfare. God describes Himself as the Commander of the Host of Heaven's Armies (Joshua 5:14), and with a mighty warrior's backing, we have little to fear.

The Bible dissects and diagnoses all of man's ails.'

"The LORD is a man of war: The LORD is his name." - *Exodus 15:3*

For this reason, God has revealed to us through the scriptures how to engage in spiritual warfare. Here are examples from Biblical characters and how they experienced spiritual warfare:

The Testing of a Righteous Man - Job (Job 1- 2)

Job was righteous, steadfast, and blameless in every way, and God was proud of him, so He blessed Job in all circumstances. You would be right if you said that this blessing was due to Jobs' obedience and steadfast desires and pursuits to please God. In the midst of these came the accuser, Satan, to the courts of God (Job 1:6-12). You know how this story goes throughout the book of Job. Here is a key takeaway: God only permitted this to happen to Job because of what the Devil said. God wanted to prove to the Devil that even if a man (Job) is stripped of all his blessings and rights from God (as Lucifer was), his heart would remain pure and loyal to God. So, you could say *God won this challenge.*

Job and his supporters.'

Question: Can you tell when God is testing you, proving the sincerity of your heart towards Him to the Devil?

Angels and Warfare in the Realm of Prayer – Daniel (Daniel 9 -10)

A Jewish boy, Daniel, was in captivity with his people under the Babylonian reign. Daniel was good at many things, such as engaging in spiritual activities. These drove him to study the scrolls, where he discovered that his people were overdue for liberation from Babylonian rule, according to the prophecies of the prophet Jeremiah. So, he fasted and prayed in the morning and evening. Little did he know that his prayers were answered the first day they went up to God. However, the answers, delivered by the Archangel Gabriel, took 21 days to get to Daniel after spiritual warfare. During these times of delay, Daniel didn't stop interceding. He remained firm in faith, and eventually, his answers came.

Question: Can you hold firm to your belief in God, trusting that He'll come through for you, even when the circumstances surrounding you seem otherwise?

Reflection

Here's a recap on understanding spiritual battles:

- Physical wars shape civilization, but spiritual warfare shapes our lives as Christians.
- The struggles we face may manifest physically, but their roots are spiritual.
- We do not wrestle against flesh and blood but against the dark forces of this world.
- Our true enemy, the Devil, has been defeated by Jesus, so we have victory over every one of his schemes.
- We were made in the image and the likeness of God, and with that comes dominion over the Earth (something the Devil envied).
- Knowing our identity in Christ Jesus brings about a knowledge of our spiritual authority over every circumstance.

Prayers

Prayer for an open and sincere heart towards God

"Search me, O God, and know my heart: Try me, and know my thoughts: see if there be any wicked way in me, And lead me in the way everlasting." - Psalms 139:23-24

Prayer for strength in battle

"Lord, strengthen me for the battles I face every day. Let me stand firm in faith and put on the full armor of God. In Jesus' name, Amen."

Prayer for Discernment

"Father, open my eyes to see the enemies' schemes. Grant me wisdom and discernment to walk in victory, always. In Jesus' name, Amen."

Prayer for Protection

"Lord, I take refuge in you. Let no weapon formed against me prosper. Preserve me in your blood in Jesus' name, Amen."

Prayer for Authority Over the Enemy

"In the name of Jesus, I resist every enemy attack. I declare victory over fear, doubt, and every temptation. I declare that I am more than a conqueror, in Jesus' name, Amen."

Chapter 2: The Armor of God as Spiritual Defense

"Finally, be strong in the Lord and in his mighty power. Put on the full armor of God, so that you can take your stand against the Devil's schemes... that when the day of evil comes, you may be able to stand your ground, and after you have done everything, to stand." - Ephesians 6:10-11, 13b

The Lord is the commander of Heaven's Army.[5]

The Lord is the commander of Heaven's Army. If you understand military ranks and positions, you know you only get promoted to higher ranks when you portray good leadership and military skills. However, the human ranking doesn't measure up to God's position. He made all things, and everything exists through Him.

However, to understand the complexity of His role, you may need to know how it works on Earth. A Commander of the Army is responsible for training and dispersing soldiers. He commands obedience, and every soldier answers to him.

As a commander, God has armor which He wields to defeat the enemies. He has passed that armor on to you. This implies that if He did it, so can you. This armor is proof that the enemy can be defeated. You've been called into the battlefield as children of God, and God's armor is your spiritual defense.

However, you should know that even in the heat of battle and having received this great armor from God, you're not left to fight alone. Paul assures you in Ephesians 4:10 to *"Be strong in the Lord, and in the power of his might,"* before putting on the whole armor of God. You cannot fight the enemy solely with your might and strength. God's strength gives you hope for victory over your foes. Following, we'll look at each piece of God's armor.

The Belt of Truth

"Stand firm then, with the belt of truth buckled around your waist," - Ephesians 6:14a

A belt is usually the last thing you consider wearing when getting dressed. It comes after every piece of the outfit is in place. However, Paul (writing in Ephesians) doesn't consider the belt the last member of a spiritual armory. In the Roman era, the belt held the pieces of the armor together. Without it, a soldier couldn't run on the battlefield nor be comfortable enough to wield his weapon. It's an essential piece of equipment that stores key ammunition for a trained soldier. If you've watched a war or military-centered movie, you'll agree that a soldier goes everywhere with his sword and knife strapped to the belt at his waist. He may not wear his complete armory if he is within his territory, but he wears the belt because it stores his weapons. Every soldier must always be alert and prepared for combat.

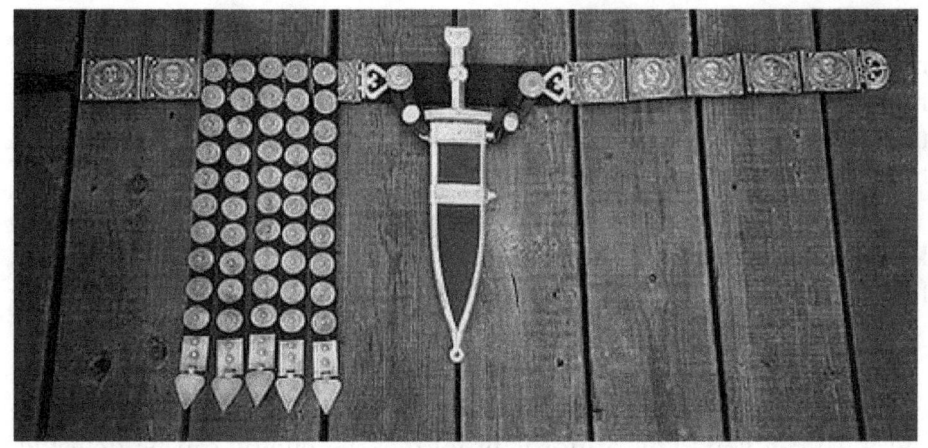

Belt of Truth.*

Paul describes the belt as a weapon of "truth." The truth is the foundation for every Christian's foundation. Without the truth, there'll be nothing to believe in or fall back on when the tides and storms appear. What is the "truth" in Christian faith? It says in John 14:6, *"Jesus answered, 'I am the way and the truth and the life..."* So, Jesus and everything to do with Him is the truth. This truth must be the center and the anchor of everything you do. The first place to find Jesus is in the scriptures. When you build your life on the truth of God's Word, you automatically strap the belt of truth to your loins.

Breastplate of Righteousness

"With the breastplate of righteousness in place," - Ephesians 6:14b

With the belt of truth strapped on, you must put on righteousness as a breastplate. The Roman breastplate is often forged from bronze, steel, or thick leather materials. It specifically covers the body's chest to the abdominal region, where the vital organs, including the heart, are located. When a soldier wears his breastplate, he fastens it to a loop or belt strap so it doesn't loosen, exposing him during battle. When the Bible says, 'Put on righteousness,' it's not what can be forged by your ability or deeds. Righteousness is a gift, not something earned or deserving when you behave justly. Remember, your righteousness to God is like a filthy rag (Isaiah 64:6).

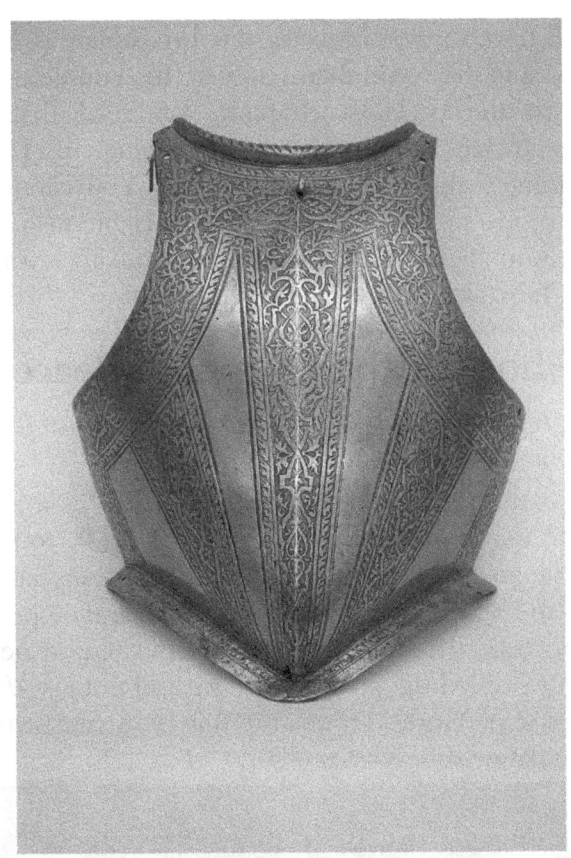

The breastplate represents righteousness.⁷

"When people work, they earn wages. It can't be considered a gift because they earned it. But no one earns God's righteousness. It can only be transferred when we no longer rely on our own works but believe in the one who powerfully declares the ungodly to be righteous in his eyes. It is faith that transfers God's righteousness into your account! Even King David himself speaks to us regarding the complete wholeness that comes inside a person when God's powerful declaration of righteousness is heard over our lives. Apart from our works, God's work is enough. Here's what David says: What happy fulfillment is ahead for those whose rebellion has been forgiven and whose sins are covered by blood? What happy progress comes to them when they hear the Lord speak over them, "I will never hold your sins against you!" - Romans 4:4-8 TPT.

Now, all you have to do to receive this breastplate is to believe God and His word, and like Abraham, it will be counted unto you for righteousness. In the previous chapter, you read that Jesus' death brought an exchange, and now, by believing in Him, you are automatically granted these packages for free! You cannot discard the first armor of truth to put on the breastplate of righteousness because it's only when you know God and His word as truth that you can believe, illustrating that these armors are rightly ordered.

Shoes of the Gospel of Peace

"and with your feet fitted with the readiness that comes from the gospel of peace." - Ephesians 6:15

With truth as the foundation and righteousness as a guard over the heart (where life issues flow from – Proverbs 4:23), you need to wear the sandals of the gospel of peace. We know that Jesus gave "The Great Commission," in Mark 16:15-20, where He grants permission and authority to permeate the world with the gospel (Good news). Are you wondering why it's called the *gospel of peace* and not just *the gospel,* and how it's an armor of God? To answer this, you must understand the purpose of a sandal or shoe for a soldier.

Wearing the correct footwear ensures that you're ready to go to war.

Can you walk a mile, two, or even ten miles without shoes? Though it may seem possible, upon considering that many injuries may be sustained, your answer will be "No." You cannot tell the condition of the road or what danger lies on it. The road to your destination may be full of rough patches and dangerous objects. This illustration is a minor scenario you can relate to. However, for a soldier, it's far worse. They'd have to travel hundreds of miles, mostly on foot, and injuries sustained would mean fatality during battle.

Knowing this, Jesus gave His disciples a simple instruction in Matthew 10:5-15. When they brought the gospel to a home, they brought peace. If that home was undeserving of this peace, Jesus said the peace instinctively returns to the disciples. So, the gospel is a channel of peace (Jesus' Peace – John 14:27) in a world filled with chaos and confusion.

As soldiers of Christ, there ought to be a readiness to proclaim the gospel at any given opportunity, even at the expense of your life. When you do, you're exercising a spiritual weapon. Jesus assures you that these opportunities will come. However, when they arrive, you may be too scared to go after them, so He says:

"Peace I leave with you; my peace I give you. I do not give to you as the world gives. Do not let your hearts be troubled and do not be afraid." - John 14:27 NIV.

Shield of Faith

"In addition to all this, take up the shield of faith, with which you can extinguish all the flaming arrows of the evil one." -Ephesians 6:16

After putting on the armor to protect your body, Paul writes that a Roman soldier still needed their shield to protect against the enemy's arrows and attacks. He mentions that your faith in God is the shield against the enemy's attacks.

What is faith? Faith is believing in something that cannot be seen. However, you can't classify merely believing as faith. For believing to be classified as faith, it needs to be converted from a passive to an active step. So, faith is believing plus action.

A shield is always needed to protect from any attacks.'

"For as the body without the spirit is dead, so faith without works is dead also."- James 2:26 KJV. To put the shield of faith to work, you cannot only believe in the word. You must act on what you believe. The scriptures are littered with Jesus repeating this phrase, *"Your faith has healed you,"* because each individual who performed daring acts had never been written of before. In the face of their struggles and great odds, they got their miracles not because they believed that Jesus could heal them but because they acted in ways that compelled the healing. Faith is a virtue and can be used as a defensive weapon. Chapter 1 exposed forms of attack on Christians by the enemy: fear, doubt, weariness, despair, and death. Your shield against these is *faith*.

When the enemy throws fear at you, raise the shield of the Word: *"God has not given me a spirit of fear; but of power, of love, and a sound mind"* (2 Tim 1:7). When the enemy throws death your way, raise your shield and declare, *"I shall not die, but live, to declare the works of the Lord"* (Psalm 118:17). You must maintain these declarations even in adversity. However, strengthening your faith is through prayer, fellowship, and equipping yourself with the word of God.

Helmet of Salvation

"Take the helmet of salvation and the sword of the Spirit, which is the word of God."- 6:17

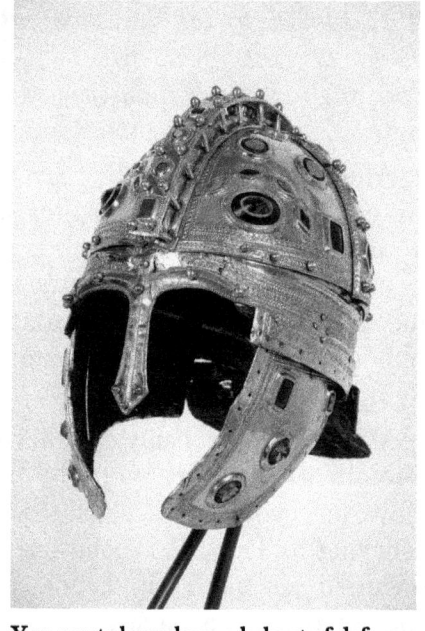

The assurance of God's salvation is an impenetrable helmet of defense you must always wear over your mind. Putting on the whole armor of God means that you must be vigilant and prepared for the enemy's attack. One way the enemy attacks is through your thoughts – *your mind is the battlefield*, and war is constantly being waged there. Salvation is not a one-time act, the only decision you made, or a futuristic event you hope for. It must be frequently exercised. If it weren't so, there would be no need for Paul to include it as an

You must always have a helmet of defense to protect your mind.[10]

armor of defense that must never be removed during the enemy's attacks. The Devil's attacks are constant. The Devil isn't happy that you're prospering. He isn't happy that you have these defensive tools and the identity of Christ. However, he knows that many Christians do not know they have these weapons at their disposal, so he uses this ignorance to his advantage. Wearing the helmet of salvation, you can exercise this scripture:

> *"Casting down imaginations, and every high thing that exalteth itself against the knowledge of God, and bringing into captivity every thought to the obedience of Christ;"* - 2 Corinthians 10:5 KJV

What is the knowledge of God? The "Truth." Whatever does not align with God's word is not welcomed in your mind. Your thoughts must be conscious and can distinguish the enemy's voice from God's voice. This can only be achieved by constantly renewing your mind to focus on your identity in Christ Jesus.

> *"And be not conformed to this world: but be ye transformed by the renewing of your mind, that ye may prove what is that good, and acceptable, and perfect, will of God."* Romans 12:2 KJV

Not all thoughts are good, not all thoughts are acceptable, and not all thoughts are perfect in accordance with the will of God. The thoughts you should have are quoted in the scripture below:

> *"Finally, brethren, whatsoever things are true, whatsoever things are honest, whatsoever things are just, whatsoever things are pure, whatsoever things are lovely, whatsoever things are of good report; if there be any virtue, and if there be any praise, think on these things."* - Philippians 4:8 KJV

As believers, this is how you should think and what should occupy your mind if you are to live victoriously.

Sword of the Spirit: Offensive Weapon in Spiritual Warfare

The previously outlined armor represents the five defensive tools.

The only *offensive* tool is the weapon of the Word - the Sword of the Spirit. It is listed last for a reason. A movie illustration can best explain this armor: when two kingdoms are at war, and the soldiers align in battle formation, whoever attacks first would likely use arrows to weaken their opponents, reduce their numbers, and create confusion.

The only offensive tool is the sword of the word.¹¹

If the opponents have good, firm battle intelligence, they can align and use a formation of shields to block the attack. The Romans were exceptional at this. They were known for their highly trained military tactics. Usually, it's not about who has more numbers but about who has better tactical strategies. When they are shielded, they can pull out their sword and attack. This sword symbolizes the power of God's word to defeat lies and temptation. A sword can be wielded in several ways, which makes a skilled soldier. Here are six ways to wield the sword of the Spirit:

Fasting and Prayer By the Word

Prayer is a powerful weapon used as an offensive and defensive tool. When wielded properly with the word of God, it becomes more powerful for pulling down strongholds.

> "The weapons we fight with are not the weapons of the world. On the contrary, they have divine power to demolish strongholds. We demolish arguments and every pretension that sets itself up against the knowledge of God, and we take captive every thought to make it obedient to Christ." - 2 Corinthians 10:4-5 NIV

In Matthew 4:1-11, Jesus was driven by the Holy Spirit into the wilderness and fasted for 40 days and nights. Fasting renders your flesh powerless, making your spirit more alive and in tune with God's Spirit. When your flesh is weak, your spirit becomes alert. You might think that 40 days is too much for one person. However, Jesus knew the Devil would come for him after previously it was declared in Matthew 3:17 that He was the son of God. He prepared so that no matter what temptations the Devil brought, which His flesh would naturally incline to (though He is God, He was in human flesh and subjected to fleshly desires), His spirit would be active enough to counter. Notice how Jesus responded to every arrow shot by the Devil. The Devil quoted the word, and Jesus responded with the Word. The Devil's words had no life, no power, and after a third blow from Jesus, he retreated from the battlefield.

Paul explains how we can pray in the spirit and according to the will of God in Ephesians 6:18

"And pray in the Spirit on all occasions with all kinds of prayers and requests. With this in mind, be alert and always keep on praying for all the Lord's people."

"Rejoice in the Lord always. I will say it again: Rejoice... Do not be anxious about anything, but in every situation, by prayer and petition, with thanksgiving, present your requests to God." - Philippians 4:4, 6 NIV.

"Rejoice always, pray continually, give thanks in all circumstances; for this is God's will for you in Christ Jesus." - 1 Thessalonians 5:16-18 NIV

Praise and Thanksgiving

"I will praise the LORD according to his righteousness: And will sing praise to the name of the LORD most high." -Psalm 7:17 KJV

Praise is an expression of gratitude and a sacrificial weapon, effective for warfare. It confuses the enemies and sets them on edge for a defeat. Do you know why praise is so powerful and is done from a place of sacrifice? Praises allow you to summon the faithfulness of God. They remind you of God's power and authority over all creation, His personality, glory, and nature. This impacts you with so much confidence to go after the Devil with the mindset that it's a battle won with God by your side.

Praise is sacrificial because it is done regardless of how you feel or how intense your circumstances are. You praise to give thanks for the good things and when things don't work out. In fact, your praise should be most powerful when things look terrible! (Acts 16:25-26; 2 Chronicles 20:21-22).

> *"Enter into his gates with thanksgiving, and into his courts with praise: Be thankful unto him, and bless his name. For the LORD is good; his mercy is everlasting; and his truth endureth to all generations."* Psalm 100:4-5 KJV

Worship

> *"God is a Spirit: and they that worship him must worship him in spirit and in truth."* – John 4:24 KJV.

Worship is an act of service (Romans 12:1). It is where you show your devotion, reverence, and loyalty through obedience. God requires His children to have, above all else, a broken and contrite heart that seeks to do His will continuously. God values this beyond anything else.

> *"For thou desirest not sacrifice; else would I give it: Thou delightest not in burnt offering. The sacrifices of God are a broken spirit: A broken and a contrite heart, O God, thou wilt not despise."* – Psalm 51:16-17 KJV.

The only way to enter and stay in worship is through the word of God. When you live a life of worship, the enemy stays defeated.

The Blood of Jesus

> *"And they overcame him by the blood of the Lamb, and by the word of their testimony..."* -Revelation 12:11 KJV

The death and resurrection of Jesus brought power through the shedding of His blood. There is ramification, redemption, and forgiveness for sins when you believe and confess God's salvation through His son Jesus with the shedding of Jesus' blood. You have been redeemed and set right with God with this one act.

The word of God is alive and active (Hebrews 4:12) in any matter you apply it to. When you approach the throne room of grace (open to every repentant sinner) and ask for mercy, you receive mercy through the blood of Jesus. This blood spoke once and continuously speaks on behalf of God's Children. In the spirit realm, the battle is between spirit and spirit, voice and voice, power and power, and, for earthly matters, blood against blood. In these matters, God's side is the greater side. When you pray, be conscious of the blood of Jesus and know that you can always plead the blood over any accusation from the enemy.

Testimonies and Declarations

"I shall not die, but live, and declare the works of the LORD."-Psalm 118:17 KJV.

You can declare God's word and His goodness privately (in a secret place) or publicly before others. Testimonies and declarations strengthen the faith of those who speak or hear them. Testimonies aren't merely words. They declare that you are a witness or partaker of an event, in this instance, a miracle or a blessing.

Have you ever witnessed a court proceeding? The witness is called to testify for or against the defendant. They are asked to declare the truth and nothing but the truth. What the witness says (declares) affects the judge's ruling. You do this when you declare God's goodness, mercies, grace, blessings, and miracles in thanksgiving and as a testimony before others.

Remember, you're constantly in a battle, and the accuser always brings false testimonies before the Father. Declaring God's word is declaring the truth and nothing but the truth. Sometimes, you may have to act in faith, declarations that you desire to become reality. The world calls these "positive affirmations." Believers call it "declaring the truth of God's Word." A good example is David's acts when he faced Goliath.

"Then said David to the Philistine, Thou comest to me with a sword, and with a spear, and with a shield: but I come to thee in the name of the LORD of hosts, the God of the armies of Israel, whom thou hast defied. This day will the LORD deliver thee into mine hand; and I will smite thee, and take thine head from thee; and I will give the carcasses of the host of the Philistines this day unto the fowls of the air, and to the wild beasts of the earth; that all the earth may know that there is a God in Israel."-1 Samuel 17:45-46 KJV

The Name of Jesus

There is much power in the name of Jesus. Jesus performed countless miracles throughout the scriptures, casting out demons, healing infirmities, and sickness. When calling on the name of Jesus with conviction, you invoke the *Person of Jesus* within and around you, and the enemy cannot stand against Jesus's mighty name (Acts 4:12; 3:6; Philippians 2:10-11).

Reflection: Building a Strong Prayer Habit

Consistency is key to maintaining a good spiritual stance. A consistent weapon that cannot be disputed is prayer. Prayer is your strongest attitude and defense against enemies. It strengthens your armor and allows you to wear the might and strength of God before engaging the enemies. Each day, you must equip yourself through studying the word, reflection, and prayer.

Each morning, start with prayer, surrendering all things to God. Tell Him to guide you through your day. Ask Him to help you remember the armor He provides and help you engage them in your daily battles. You could pray: *"Lord, help me put on your full armor today. Let your truth be a guiding light, your righteousness protection, and your word empowering in every battle. I trust you, in Jesus's name, Amen."*

As you go about your day, think about each armor and how you apply them or how you can apply them better.

Questions:

Have I experienced God's strength through prayer before?

What piece of armor do I need more understanding of?

How can I renew my mind so the word of God may richly dwell in me, and I'll be armed with scriptures when the enemy throws shade?

Chapter 3: Recognizing the Enemy's Tactics

"Be alert and of sober mind. Your enemy, the Devil, prowls around like a roaring lion looking for someone to devour." - I Peter 5:8

"Lest Satan should get an advantage of us: for we are not ignorant of his devices." -2 Corinthians 2:11 KJV

It's impossible to fight an enemy you can't see, understand, or even convinced they exist. You may not physically see the Devil because he cannot be viewed with normal vision. Yet, his ways can be studied, learned, and perceived from afar. A Soldier's advantage in battle begins when he studies his enemy's background, experience, and strategies to keep him ahead, alert, and armed with the necessary tools while preparing.

Activities in the spirit realm can be likened to a chess game – for every move, there are causes, effects, and

One of the many depictions of Satan.[11]

predictable ends. Like chess has rules, there are also rules when consciously or unconsciously dealing with the Devil.

The Devil learns all he knows by copying God's ways and patterns and has no wisdom or understanding of his own. *Nothing is new under Heaven* (Ecclesiastes 1:9), so he studies patterns and old behaviors from your ancestors or those living on Earth with the same personality and temperament and born under the same circumstances as you. He has records, takes notes, and keeps score of what may be useful in keeping people under bondage and eventually destroying them.

The Devil takes advantage of every opportunity and can use anything as a weapon. Remember, it's not about numbers on a battlefield but skills and strategies. The only reason some Christians remain unaware of the Devil's schemes and strategies is because they choose to be ignorant. God has provided deep insights on how to resist the Devil, recognize, and counter his attacks, yet He says in Hosea 4:6, "My *people are destroyed for lack of knowledge...*"

Ignorance is a disease that kills faster than the Devil. Ignorance has led many to become poor, captives, and brokenhearted. However, this is not you. God has promised that in the last days, knowledge will cover the Earth like the waters cover the sea:

"For the earth will be filled with the knowledge of the glory of the LORD as the waters cover the sea." – Habakkuk 2:14

Hence, the first step to resisting the Devil is to arm yourself with the knowledge of the glory of God. This knowledge saddles you with the truth that eventually sets you free.

"Then you will know the truth, and the truth will set you free." -John 8:32

Who Is the Enemy?

Satan may be the enemy, but that doesn't mean he operates alone. When he fell during the great war in Heaven, he fell with a third of Heaven's angels. These angels were not merely low-ranked angels under him. Some held higher ranks in Heaven than Lucifer.

What a centurion who leads an army of a hundred commands his subjects to do must be met with unfiltered obedience. How do you think Lucifer won those angels over to rebel against God? He didn't need to meet them one-on-one. He only had to convince their superior angels, and the others followed.

A fascinating story once told about how a militarized system worked. It was about how new recruits didn't have to meet the king to serve him, and they were subjects under a superior who led and commanded them. However, they must serve the king; whoever or whatever leads them otherwise should be scrutinized. Similarly, these angels' hosts willfully rebelled against God. They may not have understood Lucifer's motives behind the rebellion because the Bible records that Lucifer's thoughts were within. He may have lied to them, and they believed. It was too late when they realized they'd already picked the wrong side.

Now, imagine how these beings feel about anyone who is given salvation as a free gift.

It's recorded that there are nine Angelic hierarchies. The Bible doesn't specifically state this, but it can be deduced that most of these angels exist because they are mentioned by the major prophets in the Bible.

You should be aware of angels and their positions to understand how fallen angels occupy these angelic ranks and operate. The Bible mentions these angels:

- **Archangels (Michael and Gabriel)** – Jude 1:9; Daniel 12:1; Luke 1:19
- **Seraphim (Worship Angels)** – Isaiah 6:2-3
- **Cherubim (Guardians of God's Throne and His Holiness)** – Genesis 3:24; Exodus 25:20; Ezekiel 1:6
- **Thrones (Ophanim – The Wheels of God's throne)** – Ezekiel 1:15; Colossians 1:16
- **Dominion (Governing angels, Angels over times and seasons)** – Colossians 1:16
- **Principalities and Powers (Territorial Angels, Angels ruling over affairs of nations)** – Ephesians 6:12; Colossians 1:16
- **General Angels (Messengers, ministering angels)** – Hebrews 1:14; Psalm 91:11

As in the Kingdom of Light (GOD), each rank exists in the Kingdom of Darkness. God says in His Word that His gifts and callings are without repentance, *"For the gifts and calling of God are without repentance"* – Romans 11:29. Meaning that he doesn't take back what He's bestowed upon anyone. These entities may have lost a place in

Heaven, but it doesn't mean they lost the gifts and powers allotted to their ranks.

Whatever the Devil has or does, he copies from God, except he uses what he copies against the children of God. The Devil isn't the only one against God's children. He leads an army of rebellious angels (Revelation 12:7-9) who still actively operate with him and through people who seek consciously or unconsciously to inflict harm on others.

Here are examples of spirits and people used by the Devil:

- **Lying spirit:** In 1 Kings 22:21-22, a lying spirit deceives King Ahab through false prophets.
- **Spirit of fear and torment:** This fear attempts to cripple Christians and prevent them from exercising their God-given faith and power (2 Timothy 1:7).
- **Spirit of heaviness and depression:** This spirit erases hope and entices discouragement, sorrow, and despair (Isaiah 61:3).
- **Spirit of divination and sorcery** (witchcraft, fortune telling) (Acts 16:16-18).
- **Spirit of perversion:** This leads people to engage in sexual sins and twist the truth of God's word for personal gain (Isaiah 19:14; 1:25).
- **Manipulative and deceptive people:** A good example is King Ahab's wife, Jezebel.
- **False brethren:** Paul warns of these in Galatians 2:4-6
- **False Prophets and Teachers** (2 Peter 2:1, 2 Timothy 4:3).
- **Spirit of mammon (riches or greed):** This is the only spirit that God warns could be master over you and take His place in your life.

"No one can serve two masters. Either you will hate the one and love the other, or you will be devoted to the one and despise the other. You cannot serve both God and money." Matthew 6:24

Jesus firmly warns that in the last days, many will claim to do things in the name of Christ, and you shouldn't be ignorant of them. They appear as sheep, but within, they are devouring wolves.

"Watch out for false prophets. They come to you in sheep's clothing, but inwardly they are ferocious wolves. By their fruit, you will recognize

them. Do people pick grapes from thornbushes, or figs from thistles?" "Not everyone who says to me, 'Lord, Lord,' will enter the kingdom of heaven, but only the one who does the will of my Father who is in heaven." -Matthew 7:15-16, 21

Other scriptural references: (2 Peter 2:15; Acts 13:10)

- **Persecutors and Oppressors (Romans 9:17; Exodus 5:2)**
- **Betrayers and Deceivers (like Judas Iscariot in Luke 22:3)**
- **Lust of the eyes and flesh**

A common tool the Devil uses against Christians is the desires of the flesh, which Paul calls the old man in Ephesians 4:22 KJV.

"...that ye put off concerning the former conversation the old man, which is corrupt according to the deceitful lusts; and be renewed in the spirit of your mind; and that ye put on the new man, which after God is created in righteousness and true holiness."

The Devil uses fleshly weaknesses and desires to corrupt man and eventually destroy him. You can become a slave to the flesh if you do not flee from situations and circumstances undermining the will of the Spirit. Paul writes that the spirit and the flesh constantly war against themselves. Daily, you choose to lust after the spirit or against the spirit.

Paul warns people to resist the Devil, and he will flee, but for handling the flesh, Paul warns them to flee from youthful lust.

"Flee the evil desires of youth and pursue righteousness, faith, love, and peace, along with those who call on the Lord out of a pure heart" - 2 Timothy 2:22

He instructs you to flee youthful desires and only pursue things of the spirit. Both decisions are conscious efforts to go in the right or wrong direction.

The Enemy's Character

The Bible tags the Devil with several titles due to his operations and mode of attack. Some of these characters have been consistently portrayed by the Devil, even before the creation of the world. Here are a few of the Devil's characteristics:

Deceiver

"And no wonder, for Satan himself masquerades as an angel of light."-2 Corinthians 11:14

To deceive is to deliberately cause someone to stumble by believing what is not true for the deceiver's benefit. The Devil's purpose is to mislead people and direct them away from the Light (God). He's no longer an angel of light because he fell. Since he cannot afford to be suspected as the Devil, he disguises himself, shades, and sugarcoats the truth to look like there are alternatives to God and that God's Word can be compromised. He did this to the angels who fell with him as well as to Adam and Eve –and continues to this day. He knows there's no room for him in Heaven, so he wants to prevent as many as possible from getting there.

Accuser

"...for the accuser of our brethren, who accused them before our God day and night, has been cast down." -Revelation 12:10

An accuser accuses someone of immoral or illegal acts on the grounds of the law or what they deem right, including several accusations that may involve slander. The enemy, Satan, has taken the job of testifying day and night against believers upon himself. The Devil, Satan (meaning *accuser*), knows spiritual laws by heart. He knows that even though you've been covered by Jesus' blood after confessing unto salvation, your old self (sinful nature) may still be active, tempting you to sin and breaking God's laws. So, when you give in to his act, the Devil comes quickly with accusations in your heart and to God to dampen your faith.

Tempter

"Then Jesus was led up by the Spirit into the wilderness to be tempted by the Devil." – Matthew 4:1

The tempter makes wrong and evil look attractive and justified to those he tempts. He knows that as a human, you often make decisions under the influence of the flesh. He uses this against you by throwing darts to remove you from God's will. You must understand that not all temptations are evil. God gives His children the option to choose between His good and perfect will and sin. However, the Devil does the contrary. He tempts with evil intent to force you to give in to your fleshly desires or his desires to destroy you and others. As the accuser, he tempts you. If you fall, he accuses you of falling before God and demands that you be punished for your sins.

Destroyer

"The thief does not come except to steal, and to kill, and to destroy. I have come that they may have life, and that they may have it more abundantly."-John 10:10 NKJV.

Satan's purpose is always to destroy. He steals peace and kills joy, leaving you bare to bleed. The Devil is the author of confusion and the finisher of doubt, fear, condemnation, and death. The Devil is patient with his strategy, and one of his gateways is through families. He knows it's the first foundation of every human life and the bedrock of every flourishing society. So, he targets the foundation, for *"if the foundation be destroyed, what can the righteous do?"* (Psalm 11:3).

The Enemy's Tactics for Attack

Like in the medical field, you're taught that for a condition to be tagged as an illness, several factors must be present, such as signs and symptoms.

Signs are an external expression of what is happening internally. When consulting a physician, you're asked about the observable signs to help diagnose a presumed cause of the illness. Some illnesses run too deep and require further diagnosis through tests and scans to discern the issue before treatment is administered. Similarly, spiritually, dealing with the root cause of an attack requires seeking a spiritual diagnosis, beginning from the heart. The root causes for every spiritual ailment are:

Deception

The enemy uses lies and deceit to cover up the truth. He manipulates God's Word and convinces minds to believe there are other ways to God. Jesus said, *"I am the way, the truth, and the life. No man comes to the Father except through me."* (John 14:6). It seems straightforward and precise, right? But the Devil throws doubt – as he did to Eve:

"Is there really only one way to serve God?"

"Do you have to obey God's Word immediately?"

"Retreat to unwind from the stress of pursuing God."

The moment you reason his deceit, you've fallen into his trap. To conquer this tactic, Proverbs 4:23 says, *"Guard your heart with all diligence."* The more you meditate on God's Word, the more you're equipped with His power to divert attacks that may come through your thoughts.

Temptation

The enemy, Satan, uses succumbing to your fleshly desires to lead you astray. The desires come as urges or short-term desires to satisfy cravings, wants, or momentarily pleasures.

Remember, temptations usually serve short-term wants. It's these short-term wrong decisions that eventually come back to haunt you. Whenever people fall for their immediate urges, the Devil uses guilt and condemnation for control, so they're unable to see the grace of God extended to them for the forgiveness of their sins.

David was a victim of temptation (2 Samuel 11). He gave in to temptation by committing two sins: adultery and murder. David suffered the consequences of his actions as God's laws to the Israelites demanded "a life for a life." David's life was spared, but his child was taken instead. However, when David was confronted with his sin, he immediately repented. He didn't argue or justify his actions like many would. He was so broken that he quickly received God's forgiveness. God helped him heal and rewarded him with another son.

How do we deal with temptations? Like Jesus' defense mechanism, when the Devil tempted him, it was done through fasting, prayer, and meditating on God's Word.

Accusations

Satan doesn't only accuse believers before God. He accuses them when they give in to temptations, fleshly desires, and sin. God forgives you even when you must face the consequences of your actions. However, you may be unable to receive God's forgiveness because of the guilt and shame dealt by the Devil. Instead of receiving grace and help in times of need, you believe that the consequences of your actions are God's punishment, and you distance yourself from Him. In Luke 22:61-62, Peter was a victim of guilt because he had sinned and breached Jesus' trust. He trusted himself so much not to fall; hence, the great shame and guilt he felt after the cock crowed. Dealing with accusations means understanding that God has already forgiven you for that sin. However, you must be honest to receive it and move on with His grace. If God does not condemn you, then no one has the right to, not even you.

Discord and Division

Do you experience conflict at home, work, school, or church? Have you recently been in an argument and could not convey a correct message, leading to more misunderstanding? Have you caught yourself unconsciously backbiting or gossiping? Have you felt envious of someone? Do you have issues communicating your thoughts clearly? Do you often get misunderstood or vice versa?

Discord brings disagreement and disharmony among brethren. It's the bedrock for division. When things like malice, spite, bitterness, strife, jealousy, envy, manipulation, deception, and disagreement are left unchecked, discord is at the door, searching for openings. Whatever you do, do not settle for negative emotions over godly virtues.

> *"Don't have anything to do with foolish and stupid arguments because you know they produce quarrels. And the Lord's servant must not be quarrelsome but must be kind to everyone, able to teach, not resentful. Opponents must be gently instructed, in the hope that God will grant them repentance, leading them to a knowledge of the truth and that they will come to their senses and escape from the trap of the Devil, who has taken them captive to do his will."*
> -2 Timothy 2:23-26

Distraction

Are you experiencing forgetfulness more frequently than before? Have you had difficulty concentrating on one thing and completing it? Have you had difficulty maintaining a long conversation, especially with someone dear to you? Have you recently been making too many careless mistakes? Have you been daydreaming during a serious task? Have you been dull of hearing, struggling to listen and carry out instructions? Do you give short or delayed answers to what requires your full attention?

"A double-minded man is unstable in all his ways." -James 1:8 KJV.

Distractions are subtle, so you won't notice yourself slipping away bit by bit. The enemy uses distractions to keep you busy with everything else except the will of God. For example, Martha (Lazarus' sister) was busy with kitchen duties while her sister Mary sat at Jesus' feet, listening to the Word. Martha became angry at Mary for not helping with the distractions. However, Jesus responded that Mary chose the right way. Martha was too busy "serving" the Lord (technically, anyone might consider the best), but Jesus never directed her to do so. She chose to do the right thing at the wrong time. Consider that she wasn't privileged to have Jesus correct her. What happens then? Strife, anger, malice? Satan gives people godly responsibilities that have nothing to do with the will of God - not even the *permissive will*.

A depiction of Jesus, Mary, Martha, and Lazarus.[18]

"Martha, Martha," the Lord answered, "you are worried and upset about many things, but few things are needed – or indeed only one. Mary has chosen what is better, and it will not be taken away from her." -Luke 10:41-42

It's crucial to fight off distractions and focus on the most important thing in life: Jesus. It's the only way to overcome the Devil's tricks.

Fear and Doubt

Have you second-guessed your abilities or strong convictions? Do you have difficulties accepting compliments or praises? Do you often apologize, even when you do nothing wrong? Do you habitually talk yourself down or have occasional negative self-talk? Are you a people pleaser? Do you feel inadequate, even when you could vouch that you gave someone or something 100%?

Doubt is the worst enemy of faith. It brings fear and makes you withdraw from commitments. Doubt happens when you let distractions crawl in. When it does, it brings fear and disbelief, and eventually, you make important decisions with an unstable mind.

"But when you ask, you must believe and not doubt because the one who doubts is like a wave of the sea, blown and tossed by the wind. That person should not expect to receive anything from the Lord. Such a person is double-minded and unstable in all they do." James 1:6-8

What do you do when doubt creeps in? Remind yourself of God's faithfulness in and out of season. The possessed boy's father told Jesus, *"I believe. Help my unbelief"* (Mark 9:24). Sincerity is required whenever you're in this state, a place of accepting that you're in error and asking for help, believing God will come through. You can always rely on God's faithfulness to always help whenever you reach out to Him.

The Devil has no power over you if you do not relinquish control to him. Your daily decisions take you a step closer to God or a step into the hands of the enemy. Creating a system that watches out for you and keeps you accountable is the way out. It could be by finding a mentor, family, or friend in the faith that encourages and inspires you to keep living a Godly life. You have nothing to fear. God loves you so much, and nothing will ever change that.

Resisting the Enemy's Tactics

God has prepared and provided ways to shield you from the Devil's schemes and, most importantly, resist him. Some ways to resist the Devil are:

Be sober, alert, and vigilant (1 Peter 5:8). The Devil is always on the lookout to throw his death at you. Do not allow him to get to you in any way or through anyone.

Arm yourself with the Word of God. Let it be your daily nutrient and all that fills your heart consciously and unconsciously (Hebrews 4:12).

Let prayer be your normality. Prayer brings strength and keeps you connected to God at all times (1 Thessalonians 5:17).

Yield to the desires of the Spirit (Galatians 5:16). Usually, what your flesh wants isn't what the Spirit wants. Whenever you feel urges, search your heart to ensure they align with the word of God or are contrary. It won't be easy doing it by yourself, but you can depend on the Holy Spirit to strengthen and give you wisdom.

Reflection: Vigilance in Spiritual Warfare

Recognize Attacks

Do you have negative emotions like doubt, fear, and distractions?

Do these emotions and situations arise when you're trying to draw closer to God?

Say This Prayer: *Dear Lord, open my eyes to see the enemy's schemes. Give me grace and strengthen me with faith to overcome these temptations, in Jesus' name, Amen.*

Journaling: Spiritual Awareness and Resistance

Get a journal and reflect on these questions:

Standing firm in God's word

How familiar are you with God's word?

Do you have a list of key scriptures or memory verses you can rely on to renew your mind in times of trouble?

Prayer: *Father, give me a hunger for your word. Let your word richly dwell in me and open up your word to me as I study. Give me the strength to become a doer, in Jesus' Name, Amen.*

Seek Accountability

Do you have godly friends or good friends who can hold you accountable on your faith journey? If you do, write down their names and commit to speaking to them about your need for an accountability partner.

Prayer: *Father, surround me with Godly friends to support and encourage me in my time of need, and make me a good friend to others; in Jesus' name, Amen.*

Guard Your Heart and Mind

What content do you often listen to?

Do these contents or people leave you feeling more drained, energized, and inspired after a conversation?

Prayer: *Lord God, help me to be conscious of who and what I allow around and within me, in Jesus' name, Amen.*

The Devil is subtle, and so are his strategies – deception, temptation, accusation, doubt, division, distractions. However, God has equipped you with tools to resist his schemes. Staying vigilant, grounded in scriptures, and fervent in prayer, discerns the Devil's schemes and rightly wields God's power.

Chapter 4: The Power of Prayer and Fasting

"However, this kind does not go out except by prayer and fasting." - Matthew 17:21 NKJV.

Beyond having God's armor at your disposal, your greatest advantage in spiritual warfare is that for each attack, how or which tools to engage. The enemies do not attack one way, so why should believers only have one defense? There is hope and joy because of the Spirit of truth, and He will bring you into all truth and guide you appropriately.

Prayer can be one of your strongest weapons in spiritual warfare.[14]

However, the Spirit can only help when you are wise enough to arm yourself with sufficient knowledge. The more you know, the more the Spirit helps by aiding that knowledge with understanding. Hence, the Bible arms you with sufficient knowledge concerning spiritual matters and how to deal with the Spirit.

You've learned to wield the sword of the Spirit, the Word of God. Prayer and fasting are ways to wield the sword. Prayer is connecting and communicating with God. Fasting enhances how fast you receive God's words or blessings. When you combine both, you gain more spiritual clarity, receive breakthroughs for your life and others, and, most especially, connect deeply with God.

God shed light through several scriptures in the Bible, like Matthew 17:21. Through the scriptures, you've learned that certain enemies cannot be dealt with by prayer alone. Where the enemies are territorial (physically and spiritually), or where you have no knowledge of the spirit involved, then your flesh must be killed to fight. You must nail flesh to the cross, render it weak and futile, too futile for the enemy's use.

> *"For though we walk in the flesh, we do not war according to the flesh. For the weapons of our warfare are not carnal but mighty in God for pulling down strongholds..."* - 2 Corinthians 10:3-4 NKJV.

Jesus is the absolute example in all things – see how He prepared for the Devil's temptation (Matthew 4). He rendered himself dead in the flesh by fasting for 40 days and nights and actively praying. He taught His disciples in Matthew 17:21 the place of prayer and fasting in dealing with highly powerful demons. The Bible has many great examples of Men who engaged in prayer and fasting and saw victory, like Moses (Deuteronomy 9:15-18), Daniel (Daniel 9), Paul (Acts 14), David (Psalm 35), and many others.

Prayer

The earnest (heartfelt, continued) prayer of a righteous man makes tremendous power available [dynamic in its working]." - James 5:16b

Prayer is an integral part of Christian life. Through prayer, you exchange in the spirit due to the spiritual posture of humility before God. In exchange for humility, power is given to you in times of need. God says in His word:

"If My people who are called by My name will humble themselves, and pray and seek My face, and turn from their wicked ways, then I will hear from heaven, and will forgive their sin and heal their land." - 2 Chronicles 7:14

Prayer helps position you rightly for God's help. It aligns you with the will of the Father and invites His intervention in your life. An example is Daniel 10:12-13 when Daniel's persistent prayer led to angelic intervention in a spiritual battle. As a believer, constantly living in the will of God is vital for leading a godly life.

Prayer helps you know God's mind over matters and yields power, as in James 5:16. Righteousness is a gift from God bestowed on you through salvation in Jesus. It's an automatic grace due to surrendering your life to Jesus.

However, righteousness without prayer isn't enough to yield power in the spirit. Also, many view prayer as only communication with the Father. While that is good, there is a higher path of communication with the Father that resonates from a depth of understanding (earnest, heartfelt) - expressing His will from your heart while speaking with Him. Paul revealed that this should be the constant state of a Christian to gain victory in spiritual warfare. Heartfelt is the posture of your heart, and prayer is a channel to access the power of God within you. God is all-powerful (Omnipotent), and the more you commune with Him, the more He reveals Himself to you - the greatness of His power.

Types of Prayer

Prayers can be made by you and on behalf of others. The greatest attacks in spiritual warfare are targeted towards man's soul. The soul is most precious to God, so Paul in 1 Timothy 2:1-2 urges you to pray for "All Men," especially those in authority. You do not fight these battles alone but with the help and power of God. However, you can't receive or give this help without committing your soul and others to God for salvation. It's a great responsibility that God has entrusted to every believer, and one way is through prayer. Prayers that Christians should engage in for various outcomes are:

Intercessory Prayers

Intercession is petitioning and praying on behalf of others. It invokes God's mercy, His hand, deliverance, and intervention concerning others. It's a very powerful prayer and has proven effective on many occasions.

Throughout the Bible, God intervenes in the lives of men, even nations, because people took the time to intercede for them. The list of people who interceded in the Bible is endless, but they have one thing in common: they believed their prayers were answered even before praying.

- Abraham intercedes for his nephew Lot (Genesis 18:22-33)
- Moses intercedes multiple times for Israel (Exodus 32:11-14; 33:12-17; Numbers 14:11-20)
- King David intercedes for Israel (1 Chronicles 21:16-17)
- Elijah prayed for the widow's son, and the child came back to life (1 Kings 17:17-24)
- King Hezekiah prays for Israel's deliverance from the Assyrians (2 Kings 19:14-19)
- Nehemiah prays for Israel's restoration (Nehemiah 1:4-11)
- Job intercedes for his friends (Job 42:7-10)
- Daniel intercedes for Israel's freedom from captivity (Daniel 9:3-19; 10:12-14)
- Jesus intercedes for Peter (Luke 22:31-32)
- Jesus intercedes for His disciples and all believers (John 17:1-26)
- The church intercedes for Peter's release from prison (Acts 12:5-12)
- The Holy Spirit intercedes for believers (Romans 8:26-27)
- Paul intercedes for believers in the church (Ephesians 1:16-23; 3:14-21)
- Paul prayed for the Colossian, Philippian, and Thessalonica churches and his sons and students, Timothy and Titus.

These are only a few instances where intercession took place in the Scriptures. Abraham – the father of faith – was the first to make an intercession to God on behalf of his nephew. However, Jesus sets the ultimate example for everyone.

Abraham and Isaac.[15]

Prayers of Deliverance

Deliverance prayers free you from spiritual bondage, oppression, and demonic chains that may have kept you in captivity. The good news is that Jesus, through His sacrifice on the cross, death, burial, and resurrection, took the keys of life and death from the Devil and set the legal captives free from bondage. He has given you the same authority to trample upon serpents, set captives free, and deliver bondservants of sin. When you pray for deliverance, do it from a place of victory.

> *"Having wiped out the handwriting of requirements that was against us, which was contrary to us. And He has taken it out of the way, having nailed it to the cross. Having disarmed principalities and powers, He made a public spectacle of them, triumphing over them in it."* - Colossians 2:14-15

Jesus defeated the Devil, who kept mankind under his rule since the fall of man. Now, you can confidently pray guided, persistent prayers of deliverance for oppression or spiritual bondage, and you will be free. Remember, the enemies don't give in easily, so being persistent in prayer and praying from the blood of Jesus is crucial. It symbolizes that your sins have been washed away, and you are free from satanic bondage.

"As for you also, because of the blood of My covenant with you, I have set your prisoners free from the waterless pit."- Zechariah 9:11

Prayers of Thanksgiving

Thanksgiving is a powerful weapon that yields answers to prayers with "the peace of God." It shifts your focus from problems and circumstances to God's faithfulness.

"Be anxious for nothing, but in everything by prayer and supplication, with thanksgiving, let your requests be made known to God; and the peace of God, which surpasses all understanding, will guard your hearts and minds through Christ Jesus."- Philippians 4:6-7

Thanksgiving connects you to the will of God, stirs God's presence in your life, and strengthens your faith. Jesus taught and revealed this when He fed multitudes with five loaves and two fish. In 1 Thessalonians 5:18, Paul reminds you to be thankful to God in every situation.

The essence of a Christian is faith. When offering a prayer of thanksgiving, you're exercising and engaging your faith in God and victory over all things through Him. What a way to continuously be in a state of peace.

Persistent Prayers

Persistence portrays that you remain steady in your pursuit, even with stubborn obstacles. Jesus set a good example of what it means to be persistent. He used the parable of the widow and the ungodly judge (Luke 18:1-8). The widow's desire for justice didn't move the judge. It was her persistence. God teaches applying this principle in prayer. You shouldn't give in because you prayed once, and there is no change. Prayer should be in and out of season, regardless of the circumstances or the battle's toughness. Prayer should be continuous, without ceasing (1 Thessalonians 5:17).

Steps to an Effective Prayer

You don't only want to pray. The aim is for your prayers to be effective. Steps to guide you for effective prayer are:

Prepare Your Heart: To prepare your heart is to humbly come before God through 'mercy' with a repentant heart and the readiness to confess every sin, to receive the grace to overcome (1 John 1:9).

Be Specific: Define your prayer, clearly understand your desire, and state the struggles or battles you want to address.

Pray Scriptures: The Word of God is your sword, and prayer is a skill for wielding it. For example, Psalm 91 can be wielded through prayer for defense and protection; Psalm 51 for mercy; Psalm 41:10 reassures God's strength; Psalms 2, 35, 27, for when engaging in spiritual warfare.

Pray in the Spirit: Praying in the Spirit helps you to pray beyond human limitations and understanding. Allow the Holy Spirit to intercede and guide you (Romans 8:26).

Be Persistent: Prayer should be a habit of every Christian. Commit to consistent, fervent prayers. (1 Thessalonians 5:17)

Prayer Challenge

Is your heart burning with the desire to pray with this understanding? Then, participate in this prayer challenge. Pray these prayers consistently (daily) for one week, two weeks, and one month. Keep building the momentum nonstop; soon, it will become your lifestyle.

Week 1: Spend five minutes daily listing three things you are grateful for.

> *"Heavenly Father, I come before You today with a heart full of gratitude. I thank You for Your mercy, goodness, and faithfulness. I trust that, even on difficult days, You're working all things for my good because I love You. Father, align my heart to Your will and help me focus on Your goodness rather than my struggles. Let my life be a testament of Your grace, glory, and power, in Jesus' name, Amen."*

Week 2 and 3: Fast from your distractions (social media, non-important conversations) for about an hour. Use this time to meditate and worship.

> *"Father, I thank You for equipping me with Your strength. Life's battle can be overwhelming, but I know that I am*

more than a conqueror with You. Strengthen my spirit, Lord, sharpen my discernment, and fill me with Your wisdom. Help me hear Your voice and follow Your leading. Remove distractions that pull me away from You, and let my heart burn with passion for Your presence. Help me grow deeper in faith and be empowered to face every challenge; in Jesus' name, Amen."

Week 4: Focus on praying in the Spirit (in tongues or deep intercession) for about 20 minutes daily. Meditate on scriptures concerning God's power.

"Mighty God, I thank You for Your power at work in me to will and do of Your good pleasure. Father, let Your Spirit dwell richly in me and teach me to operate in the supernatural, to pray with faith, and to stand firm in the Spirit against every enemy attack. Let my life reflect Your glory, my prayers shake the Heavens, and my words carry power. I surrender all to You, Lord, and declare that I will work in the fullness of my calling; in Jesus' mighty name, Amen."

Fasting

Fasting can be a good physical exercise, but without the intention to get closer to God, it has no spiritual benefits. Many have understood fasting as abstaining from fleshly desires for a period, *but is that all there is to fasting?*

Throughout the Bible, when anyone decided to fast, there was serious spiritual contention over life or the lives of many. You can see how profound the impact of fasting was in the book of Daniel, chapters 9-10.

If you look through all the events of the Bible where people fasted, you realize the spiritual laws; fasting denies your flesh its wants and grants the Spirit its needs. Fasting draws you to pay attention to God and His wisdom faster than when you only pray.

Fasting shuts out your thoughts and opens your spiritual ears to hear God's voice. It allows you to pray in tune with the Spirit's desires. God is always speaking, but do you know how many times your thoughts and fleshly desires drown the voice of God? God is never silent or uninterested in your state. He is always speaking through a tree, a child, a stranger, or your friends, His word, His voice, or Spiritual leaders.

Fasting is not about gaining God's favor; it's about intentionally humbling yourself before God and getting closer to His Divinity. When you fast, it must be intended to draw closer to God, seeking His face and showing complete dependence on Him.

Examples of people who engaged in fasting in the Bible are:

Jesus spent the first 40 days and nights of His ministry fasting (Matthew 4:1-11). God had just announced Him as being His only son. Jesus knew the tempter, who now knows His identity, would come to test God's words as he did to Adam and Eve. Jesus had to prepare by fasting to get His Spirit in line with God to resist the Devil's temptations.

Esther fasted before approaching the throne of King Ahasuerus (Esther 4:16). What she was about to attempt had never been done in history, but Esther feared for the life of her people more than her life. She knew she was made Queen because God had seen the calamity ahead and granted her the privilege of saving Israel. So, she fasted, and God granted her favor in the king's sight. *"The king's heart is in the hand of the Lord, like the rivers of water; He turns it wherever He wishes"* - Proverbs 21:1.

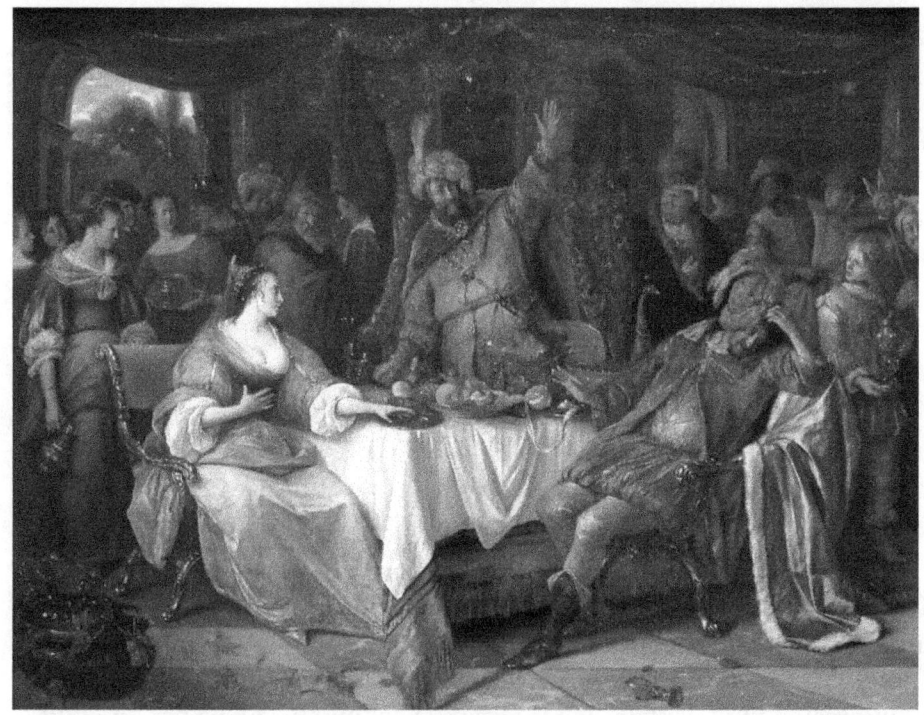

Esther and King Ahasuerus.[16]

Daniel fasted and prayed for spiritual insight into the breakthrough of Israel (Daniel 10:2-14). He had read the scrolls and realized that Israel was due for deliverance from her captors, and nothing was done about it. Daniel rendered the issue to God through fasting and prayers, resulting in a vision and receiving angelic help.

Types of Fasting

Below are the categories of fasting based on the situations:

Dry Fast (No Food and Water)

In this fast, you abstain from food and water for a period. It's usually done in times of spiritual urgency when seeking God's divine intervention. Several examples from the Bible of people who engaged in this fast are:

> "*Go, gather together all the Jews who are in Susa, and fast for me. Do not eat or drink for three days, night or day...*"- Esther 4:16

> "*For three days, he was blind and did not eat or drink anything. In Damascus, there was a disciple named Ananias. The Lord called to him in a vision, "Ananias!" "Yes, Lord," he answered. The Lord told him, "Go to the house of Judas on Straight Street and ask for a man from Tarsus named Saul, for he is praying.*" -Acts 9:9-11

The Bible states that Moses fasted for 40 days and nights and abstained from bread and water (Deuteronomy 9:9).

Complete Fast (No Food, Only Water)

In this fast, you abstain from food but sparingly from water. Your water consumption should be controlled with proper guidance and moderation. A complete fast is done when seeking spiritual strength, deep intimacy with God, and revelation. It was often practiced among the Jews. Jesus' forty-day fast is argued to be a complete fast (Matthew 4:2; Luke 4:2), meaning He may likely have taken only water and not food, perhaps why the Devil's first temptation was bread alone, not bread and water or wine.

Partial Fast (Restricting Only Certain Foods)

In this fast, you're restricted to only certain foods. However, like a complete fast, it's done guardedly, sparingly, and in moderation. Daniel engaged in a partial fast when he prayed to God. This fast aims to seek wisdom, a breakthrough, and spiritual purification.

"During those days, I, Daniel, went into mourning over Jerusalem for three weeks. I ate only plain and simple food, no seasoning or meat or wine. I neither bathed nor shaved until the three weeks were up."-Daniel 10:2-3 MSG.

Non-Food Fast (Restricting Pleasurable Activities)

In this fast, you abstain from things other than food, such as social media, entertainment, sex, etc. The aim is to help you refocus on God by eliminating distractions (1 Corinthians 7:5; Isaiah 58:6).

Spiritual Benefits of Fasting

When fasting is done correctly, it positions you to receive God's help. The benefits you gain when you fast are:

Breakthrough: Fasting lets you apply fierce pressure toward a breakthrough. With your spirit strengthened by God, you break strongholds and demonic chains. It clarifies situations that are too difficult to understand.

Humility: Fasting shifts the focus off you and makes you entirely dependent on God. It channels your desires to one thing alone: a spiritual encounter. (Psalm 35:13)

Spiritual Sensitivity: Fasting heightens your spiritual intelligence. God's voice becomes clearer and more audible to direct and guide you (Acts 13-2-3). Your spirit is strengthened to obey and be led by the Holy Spirit.

Victory Over the Flesh: Fasting helps you cut off excesses of the flesh. Your desires become subject to God's desires. You can resist temptation, overcome sinful habits, and have more tenacity to maintain self-control (Galatians 5:16).

Fasting is not only about abstaining from food. It's drawing closer to God purposefully. Whether seeking deliverance, clarity, restoration, or intercession, you must dedicate time for spiritual renewal through studying the word and prayer while abstaining from distractions or desires of the flesh.

Challenge

Decide to engage these tools in your spiritual warfare. Get your journal and a pen, and select a time to fast. Decide the timeframe – a day, a few days, a week, or a month. The idea is to start, but not to forget, and dedicate time to reading the Scriptures and prayer during the fast. Start with this simple prayer to help kickstart your decision:

> *"Lord, teach me the power of prayer and fasting. Help me to seek You with all of my heart, to trust in Your timing, and rely on Your strength in every battle, in Jesus' name, Amen."*

The aim of a Christian life hinges on a continuously growing relationship with God. Being a Christian means being dependent on God. It is the only way to overcome spiritual warfare. Praying and fasting are both ways to deepen your relationship and communion with the Father. The power everyone seeks doesn't come from these activities but from deep reliance and dependence on God.

Chapter 5: Spiritual Defense: Standing Firm Against Darkness

"Be on the alert, stand firm in the faith, act like men, be strong." - 1 Corinthians 16:13

The believer is constantly in a spiritual battle or dealing with an enemy attack. These attacks could be full-frontal assaults or rear maneuver attacks from a business partner, associate, friend, family member, or neighbor. These attacks could be the wrongful actions of someone who causes you harm. It could also result from your struggles or negative thoughts and confessions. Nevertheless, these attacks are real, and no one is excluded. This is a wicked world with a real Devil who takes pleasure in causing harm, especially to those committed to living for God and as a light to the world. As the saying goes, "For every new level, there is a Devil," and for every Devil, God has equipped you to stand firm and resist the darkness.

Knowing what the believer is up against, the Apostle Paul, in his closing remarks to the Corinthians church, admonishes them to be alert by being watchful, stand firm in the faith, and act like men by being courageous and strong. The Corinthian church held a special place in Paul's heart (Acts 18;1, 5, 11), and although he had previously taught them, he still had to exhort and help them stand firm against the darkness surrounding them.

Image depicting the Apostle Paul.[17]

The Bible's View on Darkness

"... darkness was over the face of the deep"- Gen 1:2 is the first time darkness was presented in the Scriptures. Darkness is merely the absence of light. This appeared in 22 of the 39 books of the Old Testament from Genesis, Exodus, Deuteronomy, Joshua, 1 and 2 Samuel, 1 Kings, 2 Chronicles, Job (appeared 30 times), Psalm, Proverbs, Ecclesiastes, Isaiah, Jeremiah, Lamentation, Ezekiel, Daniel, Joel, Amos, Micah, Nahum, and Zephaniah. In the New Testament, darkness appears in over 17 of the 27 books, mainly in the Gospels, Paul's Epistles, and Revelation. While on Earth, Jesus used the word 174 times in 153 verses to drive home its severity.

From Genesis, you see that whenever God the Father uses the word *darkness*, it shows the distinction between it and light. Light and day, and darkness and night. Now, consider the following Biblical meanings of darkness as gleaned from the scriptures:

Gen 1:2 – This was complete blackness before creation took place

In Matthew 27:45 and Gen 1:4- This is a physical darkness that lacks light.

In Exo 10:21, Isaiah 13:9-10, and Matthew 27:45, the darkness represents Judgement, the day of the Lord, and Jesus' death on the cross.

Job 34:22 presented darkness as the hideout of evildoers. Furthermore, in **Job 17:13,** darkness is tied to death.

Romans 2:19 shows darkness as being Ignorant

Acts 13:11 tied darkness to lack of physical sight (blindness)

Matthew 8:12 shows darkness or outer darkness as the eternal destination of the unsaved. In **Luke 22:53**, the Lord tied darkness to the evil powers of this world

Romans 13:12 and Ephesians 5:8 presented darkness as evil works and the state of the Unsaved.

Unlike the Old Testament, which views darkness as the physical opposite of light, the New Testament sees darkness through a moral compass. Not abiding in Christ's light or walking in His footsteps means walking in darkness. It shows you don't know God or understand His ways.

From the foregoing scriptures, here is a summary of darkness:

- A feeling of despair, anxiety, and fear results from spiritual isolation and wilderness
- A lack of understanding or human ignorance of divinity beyond human comprehension
- Death, sin, and evil are used to represent ungodliness, moral corruption, and the lack of the light of God.

In other contexts, darkness is a spiritual evil force of this world (Ephesians 6:12), although it has many forms, such as a jealous relative, neighbor, or evil entity. Darkness can be deceiving, showing up as a perceived good, an opportunity, a virtually kind person, etc. However attractive or repulsive those forms might seem, knowing what something represents helps you guide against it. Remember, even the Devil masquerades as an angel of light (2 Cor. 11:14). You know the truth, and the truth sets you free, so don't let the world's darkness fool you into letting down your guard.

Question: *Looking at your life holistically, what area are you experiencing darkness in, and do you need God's strength to help you stand firm?*

Be Alert

In 1 Corinthians 16:13, Paul wants the Corinthian believers to be awake, vigilant, responsible, and watchful. He desires that they watch out for evil like temptations, false teachings, wrong doctrines, and dissension lest they let down their spiritual defense and the enemy comes in with a surprise attack. As a guard watches over a prison of hardened criminals, you are exhorted to watch with the same vigilance to stay resistant to his world's darkness. The same admonition applies to every believer.

What It Means to Stand Firm

It's your unwavering commitment to Christ, even amid trials or temptations. In 1 Corinthians 16:13, 'stand firm' from the original Greek means to persevere, persist, and stand fast. "Faith" from the same verse means confidence, belief, and trust. As a believer in Christ Jesus, you ought to do the next best thing after watching: to stand fast in your trust, belief, and confidence in God and His words despite temptations or trials. You must be sure and steady, not easily swayed or wavering. It entails building and anchoring your life on the rock that will hold you during turbulent times.

Another way to stand firm is to outrightly reject spiritual oppression, sin, and temptation, knowing that Christ has won the victory on your behalf through his death on the *cross.*

> *"Then Job arose and tore his robe and shaved his head and fell on the ground and worshiped. And he said, "Naked I came from my mother's womb, and naked shall I return. The Lord gave, and the Lord has taken away; blessed be the name of the Lord." In all this, Job did not sin or charge God with wrong."* - Job 1:20-22 (ESV)

> *"Little children, you are from God and have overcome them, for he who is in you is greater than he who is in the world."* - 1 John 4:4

Notable Biblical Examples of Standing Firm

Being a child of God does not exempt you from trials and tribulations. If you feel overwhelmed by your challenges, take comfort in Christ's words: *"In the world you will have tribulation. But take heart; I have overcome the world."* (John 16:33b ESV). Notable examples from the Bible of men who stood firm when all that was left was to give up are:

Job

Job was the wealthiest man in the land. He was upright and blameless in the sight of God. Then, the Devil came to make a wager with God. To remove the edge, the Lord built around him and his household, stripped him of all he had, and tested his faithfulness to God. The Devil believed Job's faithfulness was tied to God's goodness, which he had enjoyed. So, he said to remove it all to see if Job would curse God. God agreed to the wager.

In one day, Job lost his children, vast properties, developed a skin disease, and his wife became a thorn in his side. Despite losing everything, even his friends' support, Job's faith remained unwavering in God.

> *"Naked I came from my mother's womb, and naked I will depart. The Lord gave, and the Lord has taken away; may the name of the Lord be praised.* - Job 1:21

"Though he slays me, yet will I trust in him: but I will maintain mine own ways before him." - Job 13:15

Job shows that God rewards those who stand firmly until the end despite the difficulty of trying to derail their trust in Him. Also, when you're experiencing your "Job moment," and it seems that God is nowhere to be found, trust Him and be patient; there's a reason He allowed the problems.

David and His Struggles

Most people might think David's fight with Goliath was just a stone's throw- that David never really struggled. People only think this way because they know how it ended. But imagine being a 17-year-old shepherd boy, not a man of war, standing before the giant Goliath who had seen and fought wars since his youth.

David and Goliath.[18]

Do you remember what you were like and what you did at 17? Then, imagine tossing Goliath into a scene with you in it. Is it something you would like to handle at that age? Your answer was the same as every Israelite soldier shaking in their boots, including King Saul, the tallest man in the land. For fear of losing their lives, no one would step up except David. He stood firmly against the Philistine's Goliath, and God gave him victory.

> *"David said to the Philistine, "You come against me with sword and spear and javelin, but I come against you in the name of the Lord Almighty, the God of the armies of Israel, whom you have defied.*
>
> *This day, the Lord will deliver you into my hands, and I'll strike you down and cut off your head. This very day, I will give the carcasses of the Philistine army to the birds and the wild animals, and the whole world will know that there is a God in Israel." – 1 Samuel 17:45-46*

What about David running away from King Saul because the king was after him, or his adultery that led to the death of his first child, or was it when his son Absalom wanted to usurp him for the throne? Despite these challenges, David remained firm, resolute in his trust in God, and always ran back to God when he faltered. The book of Psalms is David's many prayers because his enemies were always stronger than him and surrounded him from all sides. The Lord gave David victory because he trusted and relied on God.

Paul

Paul was an apostle of Christ and one of the greatest missionaries who wrote about half of the New Testament. Before his salvation, while he was Saul, he persecuted the church. You would think that becoming a child of God should offer you a stress-free life with no hitch. Right? Well, hear it from Paul:

"Five times I received from the Jews the forty lashes minus one.

Three times I was beaten with rods, once I was pelted with stones, three times I was shipwrecked, I spent a night and a day in the open sea,

I have been constantly on the move. I have been in danger from rivers, in danger from bandits, in danger from my fellow Jews, in danger from Gentiles; in danger in the city, in danger in the country, in danger at sea, and danger from false believers.

I have labored and toiled and have often gone without sleep; I have known hunger and thirst and have often gone without food; I have been cold and naked" - 2 Corinthians 11:24-27

In all these trials, Paul kept praising and trusting God.

Peter the Apostle

Peter was strong-headed as a follower, lost faith walking on water to meet Jesus, and denied Jesus thrice. You would think that after denying Jesus, Peter would pack up and leave town as most would have done in the same situation. However, he did the opposite - he remained and persevered through his struggles and later became the leader of the twelve Apostles. He was an Apostle who preached the gospel when the church was heavily persecuted and the only one mentioned in the Bible whose shadow healed the sick (Acts 5:15).

The Apostle Peter in prison, praying to God.[19]

There will always come a time when your faith will be tested, when the evil one will challenge the word you have received. In the words of Jesus over Peter, *"Your Faith would not fail, for you will stand still and would see the salvation of the Lord."* All that is required is that you hold on to trust and believe in God.

Strategies for Standing Firm Against Darkness

Your faith will be tested as a believer in a spiritually saturated world. Then, you must stand firm. The enemy knows how to target you when you are at your weakest.

Strategies to help you stand firm against the darkness are:

Recognizing Spiritual Attacks

The enemy is constantly waging attacks on everyone, yet only a few are aware due to the subtle manner of the enemy's attacks. The enemy has devised ways that a believer could overlook. So, the believer might have the wrong notion about spiritual attacks, believing them to be crazy or dramatic. While the believer is hung up on this idea, he lets down his guard, and the enemy pours attacks on him. Only those who can discern will be able to tell when the enemy is at work.

These attacks could come as spiritual blindness, keeping believers unaware of the truth, their identity in God, and what Christ's death achieved for them.

> *"Whose minds the god of this age has blinded, who do not believe, lest the light of the gospel of the glory of Christ, who is the image of God, should shine on them."* - 2 Corinthians 4:4 NKJV

The Devil brings distraction to keep you from studying the word, praying, and being in the company of other believers who would sharpen your faith. Since you are visually oriented, the enemy attacks through what you see, hear, or listen to. The enemy comes after Christians in many ways. However, the first step to successfully stand against this world's darkness is recognizing an attack from the Devil. You must acquaint yourself with how the enemy operates. This understanding is not far-fetched, as the Devil's different strategies are exposed throughout the scriptures. The Devil has nothing new under his sleeves. His ways have been revealed to every believer.

Trust That God Is in Control

> *"When you pass through the waters, I will be with you; And through the rivers, they shall not overflow you. When you walk through the fire, you shall not be burned nor shall the flame scorch you."* - Isaiah 43:2

> *"You will keep in perfect peace all who trust in you, all whose thoughts are fixed on you! Trust in the LORD always, for the LORD God is the eternal Rock."* - Isaiah 26:3-4

Jonah and the fish.[30]

Like Jonah in the belly of the Fish, the three Hebrew men thrown into the furnace fire, or the Lord's disciples caught in the storm, it doesn't matter how overwhelming the storms might be; God is in control and will always bring you out on the other side if you trust Him. He is right there to walk you through any darkness. The Psalmist, wanting to paint a picture of the depth to which God is willing to go, asked the following questions:

> *"Where can I go from your Spirit? Where can I flee from your presence?"*
>
> *"If I say, "Surely the darkness will hide me and the light become night around me,*
>
> *even the darkness will not be dark to you; the night will shine like the day, for darkness is as light to you."* – Psalm 139:7,11-12

Abide in His Word

The word of God is a light and a lamp on your path. You cannot stumble in the dark with it because it will always guide you to come out without banging your foot against the stone. The word is alive and active, and there's no way you can ever go wrong when you abide by it.

"Then Jesus said to those Jews who believed Him, "If you abide in My word, you are My disciples indeed. And you shall know the truth, and the truth shall make you free." - John 8:31-32

The following are ways to help you abide in His word:

Listen and meditate on scriptures often. Use the audio Bible tool to achieve this goal.

Talk to yourself by speaking God's word over your life and declaring His promises.

Have a journal where you can write scripture for easy meditation.

Put on the Whole Armor of God

Ephesians 6:10-24 perfectly sums up the battles in this world and what is expected of a Christian to stand firm. The Apostle Paul admonishes that you put on the armor of God, not some of it but the whole armor, so that you can stand against the barrage of the enemy and keep standing.

Every piece of God's armor points to your identity and inheritance in Christ. Putting it on means awakening the consciousness of who you are and what you have in Christ. This truth solidifies that no darkness will get the best of you in whatever form it comes at you. Reread Chapter 2 of this book to be reminded of the full armor you have been equipped with by God.

Prayer

Prayer is a powerful tool for standing firm against darkness. You don't pray to bend God's hands to work in your life, but an act of your faith and trust in Him and His ability to hear and strengthen you. Regular prayers in times of assault can help you remember that God is with you, which helps to keep your heart steady in Him.

Building a Support System for Community

Everyone was designed to be in a family, to make connections, thrive, and go through life together. The slogan *"no man is an Island"* is true when standing firm against darkness because you can't go at the enemy by yourself. You must learn to rely on others of like-minded faith and passion to withstand the enemy's assault.

A community of believers will build and increase your resilience and help you overcome the stresses and challenges. It could be a Bible study group, a friend in faith, or the church family who constantly speaks faith and hope in your direction.

> *"Two are better than one, because they have a good reward for their toil. For if they fall, one will lift up his fellow. But woe to him who is alone when he falls and has not another to lift him up! Again, if two lie together, they keep warm, but how can one keep warm alone? And though a man might prevail against one who is alone, two will withstand him - a threefold cord is not quickly broken."* (Ecclesiastic 4:9 - 12 ESV)

"Not neglecting to meet together, as is the habit of some, but encouraging one another, and all the more as you see the Day drawing near." - Hebrews 10:25 ESV

In this community, some individuals have walked the same path. Learn and be guided by them to help you stand firm.

Act Like Men and Be Strong

Paul's exhortation is to be brave, spiritually mature, and courageous in the darkness. This charge wasn't only to the Christian believers but to everyone in the faith. Remember, you can do all things not because you are strong in yourself but because you're strong in Him, and He is the one who strengthens you (Philippians 4:13).

> *"Have I not commanded you? Be strong and courageous. Do not be afraid; do not be discouraged, for the Lord your God will be with you wherever you go."* - Joshua 1:9

> *"Finally, be strong in the Lord and in his mighty power."*
> - Ephesians 6:10

Reflection

Having grasped what it means to stand firm and defend your spirit against this world's darkness, the following daily exercises ensure you stand firm:

Say a prayer before the start of your day. You can say the following:

"Lord, today I stand firm in Your strength. Equip me with Your armor, fill me with Your Spirit, and guide me in Your truth. I declare that no weapon formed against me will prosper. In Jesus' name, Amen."

Select a scripture verse to memorize throughout your day and ponder it, making it personal. You don't have to wait for the Devil to knock at the door of your mind before you start. In addition, endeavor to give God praise, thanking Him for His goodness and faithfulness you enjoy.

Consider your life retrospectively and determine areas where you are wavering, feeling most tempted, or being attacked. Write them out and apply the strategies for standing firm.

If toxic and negative individuals are around you, draining your energy and leaving you emotionally worn out, you must set boundaries by limiting the time you spend with them or avoiding emotional ties with them. Ask God daily for discernment and protection from these individuals. Say prayers like: *"Lord, grant me wisdom and strength to guard my heart and energy. Fill me with Your peace and shield me from negativity. In Jesus' name, Amen."*

Consciously declare God's word over your life and your family's as well. Picture being clothed in the armor of God, and no evil shall befall you, nor will any plague come near your dwelling. Make this your morning routine before going about your day.

Be conscious of your physical and spiritual environment. Remove what might give the enemy an inroad into your life. Nothing just happens. So, you must be mindful of the movies you watch, the music you listen to, the company you keep, and the words you hear. Your eyes and ears are among the major gateways into your heart. You must guard your heart and scrutinize what you allow around you. Declare this: *"I consecrate my home and life to the Lord. No darkness has authority here, for this place belongs to God."*

Chapter 6: Overcoming Curses and Generational Bondage

"Christ has redeemed us from the curse of the law, having become a curse for us (for it is written, "Cursed is everyone who hangs on a tree") so that the blessing of Abraham might come upon the Gentiles in Christ Jesus, that we might receive the promise of the Spirit through faith." - Galatians 3:13 – 14 NKJV.

Curses are words, spiritual strongholds, or influences negatively impacting individuals, families, or generations. They are self-inflicted (living in sin and unbelief), passed down from generations, or placed on one person by another.

Curses can exist in your life, but it's in your hands to break them down.[n]

The opposite of curses are God's blessings, which are superior. So, many Christians today still think that they can never be free from a curse, regardless of whether it's a family curse, patterns, or those placed on them by people. This chapter shows you how to break free from curses and generational bondages.

The passage in Galatians 3:13-14 emphasizes the freed state of the believers in Christ from the curse of the law and generational bondages. Christ's sacrifice on the cross (becoming a curse for your sake) made you free from any curse that may have kept you bound. Through His death on the cross, you have received the divine power to break free from a curse, limitation, or stronghold. You are fully authorized to live freely in Christ without condemnation as long as you believe in Him. Curses can be viewed as negative declarations or a wish that evil, harm, destruction, or calamity befalls a person.

You may have watched movies or heard stories about how a curse is directed at someone or a particular group and the diabolical undertones or supernatural implications accompanying them. From the Old to the New Testament, the Bible illustrates many of these scenarios and how these people broke free from those curses, like Balaam's attempt to curse Israel, which God turned into a blessing (Numbers 22).

Curses don't come from a place of good intentions. It hinders and makes life difficult for the cursed.

They usually exist in different forms:

Spoken curses, examples are Genesis 49:3-4 when Jacob laid a curse on his first son Reuben for sleeping with his concubine Bilhah, Genesis 3:14-19, the curses God pronounced on Adam, Eve, and the serpent for disobeying Him.

Magic, spells laid on individuals by witchcraft activities to bewitch and curse them.

Occult practices aimed at harming individuals.

Self-imposed curses, like speaking negatively about yourself, like "I'm not good enough," "I'm dumb and don't deserve God's love."

Curses can naturally fulfill themselves once they've been pronounced, which is evident in Mark 11:13-21, when Jesus, in the presence of His disciples, cursed a fig tree for appearing as though it had fruit, when it was barren. Later, when they passed by the fig tree, Jesus had cursed; verse 21 says:

"And Peter, remembering, said to Him, "Rabbi, look! The fig tree which You cursed has withered away."

However, the only exception to this self-fulfilling power of curses is when there is no cause for the curse, as in Proverbs 26:2b AMP.

"So, the curse without cause does not come and alight [on the undeserving]."

What Are Generational Curses?

Generational curses are curses that lead to generational bondage that continuously affects an entire lineage. These curses cause a repeated pattern of sin, dysfunction, or suffering, usually passed through generations. They can be caused by sin, covetousness, grievous mistakes committed in the past, covenants made with the Devil by forefathers, or past disputes with people (especially people with demonic influence or authority). Financial struggles, marital issues, barrenness, anger, fear, or addiction are examples of generational bondages faced by many today. The Bible describes it as the consequences of the sin of idolatry affecting several generations.

"You shall not bow down to them nor serve them. For I, the Lord your God, am a jealous God, visiting the iniquity of the fathers upon the children to the third and fourth generations of those who hate Me." - Exodus 20:5 NKJV.

"The LORD then passed in front of him and called out, 'I, the LORD, am a God who is full of compassion and pity, who is not easily angered and who shows great love and faithfulness. I keep my promise for thousands of generations and forgive evil and sin; but I will not fail to punish children and grandchildren to the third and fourth generation for the sins of their parents." - Exodus 34:6-7 GNB.

Genesis 9:21-27 narrates how one of Noah's sons, Ham, incurred generational curses on Canaan. The passage explained that he came into the tent and saw his father drunk and naked. Instead of doing right by covering his father's nakedness, he (Ham) chose to make a mockery of him and called his brothers to see him in his drunken state.

"When Noah awoke from his wine [induced stupor], he knew what his younger son [Ham] had done to him... So, he said: "Cursed be Canaan [the son of Ham]; A servant of servants, he shall be to his brothers." - Genesis 9:24-25 AMP

Due to his misconduct, Ham made his father pronounce curses on his son Canaan, leading to generational bondage for the descendants of Canaan.

2 Kings 5:26-27 also shows how Elisha the prophet cursed his servant, Gehazi, and his generation with leprosy due to his greed and lust for earthly possessions.

"Therefore, the leprosy of Naaman shall cling to you and your descendants forever." And he went out from his presence leprous, as white as snow." - 2 Kings 5:27 NKJV

Manifestations of Curses and Generational Bondage

The first step to overcoming and breaking free from curses and generational bondages is understanding their manifestations.

Some include:

Emotional Struggles

Curses and generational bondage can manifest in unexplained anxiety, depression, and fear of the unknown in a person's life. Genesis 4:8-13 shows an account of how Cain and part of his generation lived a life of emotional turmoil after God cursed him for killing his younger brother Abel.

"So now you are cursed from the earth, which has opened its mouth to receive your brother's blood from your hand." - Genesis 4:11.

Cain slaying Abel.[22]

Although Cain's generation later broke free from the curse, a lineage of great men began to walk with God, beginning with Enoch. 1 Peter 5:7 TLB provides a remedy to anyone facing emotional struggles. It says, *"Let Him (God) have all your worries and cares, for He is always thinking about you and watching everything that concerns you."*

Spiritual Oppression

Curses and generational bondages could hinder you from connecting and communicating properly with God or receiving answers from Him, like Daniel's answered prayers were withheld by the Prince of Persia. Spiritual attacks, feelings of darkness, recurring temptations, and lust are some ways these curses can be manifested in a person's life. Examples of spiritual oppression are observed in families where young men tend not to live beyond a certain age, or the women experience consecutive miscarriages, while some find it extremely difficult to conceive and bear children.

Relationship Issues

Curses could lead to unstable marriages or relationships. There are families with repeated patterns of divorce, estrangement, and disagreements, and until these curses are broken, the victims may never experience blissful relationships.

In 1 and 2 Samuel, David's family and lineage had a repeated pattern of adultery, lust, and relationship issues. David was born out of adultery, and he committed the same adultery with Bathsheba (Uriah's wife). His sons, Ammon and Absalom, were very unstable and did abominable things in the sight of God. Solomon followed suit with 700 wives and 300 concubines.

Financial Difficulties

This is a common manifestation where families and individuals continue to experience a pattern of financial constraint. It appears in two ways: when all hard work and efforts to get out of poverty yield no success, and a recognized pattern of laziness, making it impossible for any family member to break free from the strongholds of debt or manage their resources properly to incur wealth.

Anyone willing can break free from these unwanted curses, generational bondages, and never-ending struggles. Jesus Christ became the ultimate curse bearer when He died on the cross for all. He broke the power and curse of sin and death and freed you entirely.

"So, there is now no condemnation awaiting those who belong to Christ Jesus... For the power of the life-giving Spirit (and this power is mine through Christ Jesus) has freed me from the vicious circle of sin and death." - Romans 8:1-2 TLB.

"Therefore, if the Son makes you free, you shall be free indeed." - John 8:36 NKJV.

As a believer in Christ Jesus, you're no longer defined by your past or family history but by your new identity in Christ.

"Therefore, if anyone is in Christ (that is, grafted in, joined to Him by faith in Him as Savior), he is a new creature (reborn and renewed by the Holy Spirit); the old things (the previous moral and spiritual condition) have passed away. Behold, new things have come (because spiritual awakening brings a new life)." - 2 Corinthians 5:17 (AMP)

As a new creature and firm believer in Christ, the Holy Spirit empowers you to live in freedom. You can discern spiritual strongholds and walk in victory (2 Corinthians 3:17).

Practical Ways to Overcome Curses and Generational Bondage

You can take several steps to overcome these curses and generational bondages:

Pray to the Holy Spirit to reveal areas of bondage or curses in your life and family. You may need to sit and reflect on a family pattern you noticed in the past years indicating spiritual strongholds. The Holy Spirit will show you these generational bondages if you are sincere and ask in faith. According to Reinhard Bonnke, the popular evangelist, *"The Holy Spirit is a healing spirit. When the Holy Spirit is present, anything is possible."*

After the Holy Spirit has uncovered these patterns, the next step is to boldly renounce ungodly beliefs, previous sinful involvements, or negative relationships from the past. Ungodly covenants or agreements with the Devil that your forefathers or the family made should also be renounced.

Forgive those who have hurt you in the past. Unforgiveness can be a significant gateway for the enemy to enter a person's life and keep him perpetually in spiritual bondage. It makes you give in to the lies and tricks of the Devil. However, once you can forgive and let go, as Christ forgave you, the Holy Spirit enters your heart and replaces the Devil's lies with the truth and life of God's word.

"Be gentle and ready to forgive; never hold grudges. Remember, the Lord forgave you, so you must forgive others." - Colossians 3:13 TLB.

Applying the blood of Jesus. In spiritual warfare, the blood of Jesus (the lamb of God) is one of the most powerful weapons you can use in overcoming curses and generational bondages. Why? It's declaring the blood of Jesus over your life and family. It breaks every stronghold, cleanses, and protects you from your adversary (the Devil) and his agents.

"And they overcame him (the Devil) by the blood of the Lamb, and by the word of their testimony." - Revelation 12:11a NKJV.

Replace lies and negative beliefs with scriptures that declare God's faithful promises over your life. Instead of wallowing in self-defeat, fear, or believing that you can't do anything and will always struggle, you replace those negative thoughts by boldly saying and believing God's word and perspective of you.

"I can do all things through Christ who strengthens me." Philippians 4:13 NKJV

"He made Christ who knew no sin to (judicially) be sin on our behalf so that in Him we would become the righteousness of God (that is, we would be made acceptable to Him and placed in a right relationship with Him by His gracious lovingkindness)." - 2 Corinthians 5:21 AMP

Now, you also consciously declare, "I'm the righteousness of God through Christ Jesus."

Commit to a new legacy. You are now a new creature in Christ, so you are expected to create a new legacy for yourself and your family. Here's how to do this:

Live a life of faith and obedience to God, then believe and receive His numerous blessings. These actions ensure the negative cycles are completely broken. (2 Corinthians 9:8-10, Numbers 6:24-26)

You have to teach the next generation about the truth of God's word and how they can live a life of freedom by presenting yourself as a model of that freedom.

Notable Biblical Examples of Freedom from Curses

The Bible has demonstrated that breaking free from curses and generational bondages is possible. The ultimate way is to confess your sins and believe in Jesus Christ, who became a curse to set you free from all curses and generational bondages. (Colossians 2:14-15). A few other examples from the scriptures are:

The Israelites in Egypt

The Israelites had been slaves in Egypt for hundreds of years after the death of Joseph and the arrival of a new Pharaoh who did not respect God and His people. Exo. 12:31-42 tells of how God broke the curse of slavery from the Israelites and led them out of Egypt into freedom through Moses.

The Israelites in Egypt.[28]

"Now the sojourn of the children of Israel who lived in Egypt was four hundred and thirty years... And it came to pass at the end of the four hundred and thirty years, on that very same day, it came to pass that all the armies of the Lord went out from the land of Egypt... It is a night of solemn observance to the Lord for bringing them out of the land of Egypt. This is that night of the Lord, a solemn observance for all the children of Israel throughout their generations." - Exodus 12:40-42 NKJV.

Daniel

Daniel was described as a man with an excellent spirit, yet his people (the Israelites) were under captivity in Babylon for seventy years, under a harsh king who worshipped idols. Daniel knew that his people were under a curse from God, hence the reason for their captivity.

"Yes, all Israel has transgressed Your law, and has departed so as not to obey Your voice; therefore, the curse and the oath written in the Law of Moses the servant of God have been poured out on us, because we have sinned against Him." - Daniel 9:11 NKJV

So, Daniel confessed the iniquities of his people to God, fasted and prayed fervently for the curse to be overturned, and his people were freed from the curse of captivity. It happened just as he prayed.

Esau

Esau was a notable person who broke free from the curse placed on him by his father after Jacob had craftily taken his blessing (Genesis 27:27-40).

After Isaac had blessed his second son, Jacob, in place of Esau, his firstborn, there was nothing left but curses for Esau, who had arrived later. Remember, the opposite of curses are blessings. However, the scriptures showed Esau and his generation to be very successful years later, implying that he broke the curses and lived a victorious life Genesis 36 and 37)

Paul

Acts 9:1-19 narrates the story of Paul (previously Saul), the chief persecutor of Christians in 35 AD. He was on his way to Damascus for his routine persecution tours when he experienced a great light from Heaven that blinded him. It was as though a spell was cast on him. The

Lord directed him to Ananias, who prayed for him, and the spell was removed after he confessed his sins, accepted Christ, and was baptized.

> *"Immediately, something like scales fell from Saul's eyes, and he could see again. He got up and was baptized."* - Acts 9:18 NIV.

Reflection

Renunciation is one way to break curses and bondages. However, you cannot renounce curses that you don't know exist. So, you should reflect deeply on your and your family's lives. Write down where you have observed repeated struggles or family patterns dating back to previous generations. For example, in a case of premature death, ask yourself questions like "Who else has died prematurely in the family, extended and nuclear? How long has this been happening? Is this peculiar to my mother's or my father's lineage?" Write down the answers before renouncing them in prayer.

Prayer for Renunciation

> *"In Jesus' name, I renounce every form of curse, sin, and stronghold (name them) that has held me bound and affected my family. I break its power by the authority of Jesus Christ. I declare that I am a new creature free from bondage and redeemed by the blood of Jesus, Amen."*

After saying this prayer, believe that you are victorious and walk in this victory by continuously speaking God's truth over your life and family.

> *"No weapon formed against you shall prosper, and every tongue which rises against you in judgment, you shall condemn... this is the heritage of the servants of the Lord, and their righteousness is from Me," says the Lord."* - Isaiah 54:17 NKJV

Family Deliverance Prayer Sessions

Families under the influence of generational bondages and curses should come together in prayer and ask God to reveal and break strongholds affecting their households. Each family member can take turns praying as the Holy Spirit leads them to specific areas where they have seen struggles or repeated patterns.

Thereafter, God's promises should be declared over the family.

> *"Here am I and the children whom the Lord has given me! We are for signs and wonders in Israel from the Lord of hosts, who dwells in Mount Zion."* - Isaiah 8:18 NKJV.

> *"But for those who honor the Lord, his love lasts forever, and his goodness endures for all generations."* - Psalms 103:17 GNT.

Read and meditate on scriptures like Joshua 24:15, Psalm 128:3-4, and many others that show God's promises, His love, blessings, and protection over your family. Declare the blood of Jesus and anoint the home as an emphatic symbol of consecration to God.

Living in freedom and overcoming these curses and generational bondages is like a process based on faith in the finished work of Christ, obedience to God's word, and reliance on the Holy Spirit.

Overview of Generational Blessings

After going over these steps, the next thing is to make a total shift in your heart by believing that the curses have been broken. This shift is entirely removing your focus from the curses and bringing them to the more superior generational blessings that God has for you and every family that believes in him.

> *"For God hath not given us the spirit of fear; but of power, and of love, and of a sound mind."* - 2 Timothy 1:7 KJV

You and your family can deeply study Biblical families who enjoyed God's favor and blessings. These blessings were given by God and passed on from one generation to another. For instance, Abraham was known to have faithfully walked with God (Genesis 12:2-3), and he received generational blessings that passed on to his son, Isaac (who sowed in a dry land but was still successful - Genesis 26-27), Jacob his grandson, and many generations after him.

> *"I am the God of Abraham, the God of Isaac, and the God of Jacob? God is not the God of the dead, but of the living."* - Matthew 22:32 NKJV

The God of Abraham, the God of Isaac, and the God of Jacob signify that they were a generation who enjoyed sustained blessings from God. After Abraham had obeyed God and almost sacrificed his son, Isaac, God said to him:

"I will surely bless you and make your descendants as numerous as the stars in the sky and as the sand on the seashore. Your descendants will take possession of the cities of their enemies... and through your offspring all nations on earth will be blessed, because you have obeyed me." - Genesis 22:17-18 **NIV**

David's family also enjoyed generational blessings from God. He and his sons maintained Israel's kingship and possessed power and vast wealth from God. To crown it all, Jesus Christ, our Lord and Savior, came from the lineage of David. They were indeed a blessed generation.

"My covenant I will not violate, nor will I alter the utterance of My lips.

Once (for all) I have sworn by My holiness (My vow which cannot be violated); I will not lie to David.

His descendants shall endure forever and his throne (will continue) as the sun before Me. "It shall be established forever like the moon, and the witness in the heavens is ever faithful." - Psalm 89:34-37 **AMP**

Be encouraged by the blessings and favor these families received from God. You'll see their manifestations in your life when you desire and believe these blessings. One way to tap into these generational blessings is by having a legacy of faith chart for the family. Write down intentional actions through which these spiritual blessings from God can be passed on to future generations – actions like consistently studying and teaching God's word, praying without ceasing, and living righteously.

Chapter 7: Protecting the Family Through Faith

"By faith Noah, being divinely warned of things not yet seen, moved with godly fear, prepared an ark for the saving of his household, by which he condemned the world and became heir of the righteousness which is according to faith." – Hebrews 11:7 NKJV

The family unit is essential to God's plan and purpose for mankind. He created and intended this masterpiece to be a household consisting of a man and a woman coming together as husband and wife (marriage) and subsequently giving birth to Godly children (a reward from God). *"For this reason, a man shall leave his father and his mother, and shall be joined to his wife; and they shall become one flesh."* – Genesis 2:24 AMP. The Bible gives various instances that show how much God values "Family." A notable example is in Matthew 2:13-15, where God directed Joseph to lead his family to safety when their lives were under threat from King Herod.

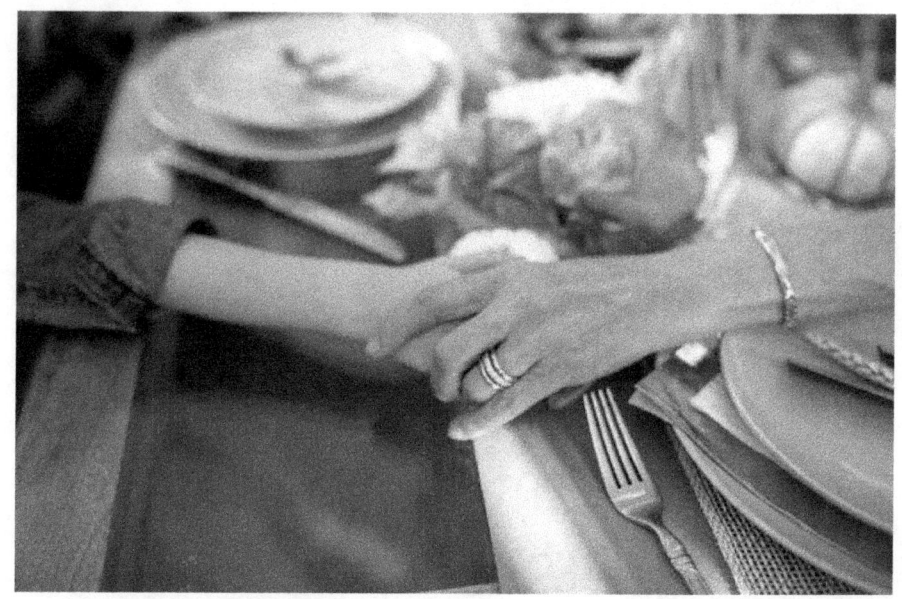
A family united through faith and prayer can overcome anything.³⁴

A family built on faith in God is well fortified against the enemy's spiritual attacks. Hebrews 11:7 shows how Noah saved his family through his faith in God. Faith was established as a virtue to be used as a weapon of defense against the enemy's attack. So, it's advantageous to any family that wields it against the enemy. God created the concept of family as society's core foundation, intended to reflect His love and unity, and the enemy, knowing this significance, poses all manner of threats and attacks towards it. The scripture recorded that once a foundation is destroyed, nothing can be done for the building (Psalm 11:3). The enemy targets this foundation through internal and external influences from the world to harm or divide the family. Faith in God is the shield against them.

The Devil uses many strategies to attack and attempt to frustrate families. The most common ways are:

Breakdown of Communication and Relationship

Communication is the bedrock of a strong relationship or family. When there's a gap, many things can go wrong. The enemy uses this as an attack to affect the peace of the home, the spirit of love, togetherness, unity, and purpose in God. This was not God's intention when he created this beautiful institution. The Bible shows in Genesis 11 how a communication breakdown affected a people united like a family to build the tower of Babel.

The Tower of Babel.³⁵

"But the Lord came down to see the city and the tower which the sons of men had built... and the Lord said, "Indeed the people are one and they all have one language, and this is what they begin to do; now nothing that they propose to do will be withheld from them... Come, let us go down and there confuse their language, that they may not understand one another's speech." So, the Lord scattered them abroad from there over the face of all the earth, and they ceased building the city." – Genesis 11:5-8 NKJV

Exposure to Harmful Influences

Humans are influenced by their senses, especially what they hear and see. The enemy knows this, so he continuously presents you with images and words that disagree with God's plan and word. They are regarded as external influences because you ingest them from the world's view and sounds. When Christians constantly surround themselves with these negatives, they take form in their hearts, affecting their dealings with life and people.

The Devil disguises these external threats as good and acceptable societal norms. For example, ungodly social media content and trends and cultural beliefs that are not in line with God's principles, and movies and music that don't align with God's word. The Devil aims to get the family to believe these lies and veer off God's plan and purpose.

The story of Dinah, Jacob's daughter, exemplifies this in Genesis 34. Dinah was defenseless against external influences when she went out to see the daughters of the land, and she was violated.

> *"Now Dinah, the daughter of Leah, whom she had borne to Jacob, went out to see the daughters of the land. And when Shechem the son of Hamor the Hivite, prince of the country, saw her, he took her and lay with her, and violated her."* - Genesis 34:1-2

The story continues, but the focus is on the external influences Dinah was exposed to and how they affected her.

Generational Sin Patterns

The Devil attacks the family by setting up generational sin patterns. The Devil always introduces these patterns to every generation. As members from different generations yield to it, it becomes familiar and mistaken as a norm or a family trait, giving room for the enemy to control the family. Until a family member recognizes it as the Devil's strategy and stands up against him, armed with the Armor of God, the pattern continues, and the family remains in bondage.

Abraham's family was notable in the Bible because of its history of generational sin. It all began in Genesis 12:10-20 in which the Bible tells how he lied about Sarah being his sister.

> *"And Pharaoh called Abram and said, "What is this you have done to me? Why did you not tell me that she was your wife?... Why did you say, 'She is my sister'? I might have taken her as my wife. Now, therefore, here is your wife; take her and go your way."* - Genesis 12:18-19 NKJV

This sin continues down the lineage to Isaac, his son, who lied about Rebecca, his wife.

> *"And the men of the place asked about his wife. And he said, "She is my sister," for he was afraid to say, "She is my wife," because he thought, "lest the men of the place kill me for Rebekah, because she is beautiful to behold." Now it came to pass, when he had been there a long time, that Abimelech, king of the Philistines, looked through a window and saw, and there was Isaac, showing endearment to Rebekah, his wife. Then Abimelech called Isaac and said, "Quite obviously, she is your wife; so how could you say, 'She is my sister'?" Isaac said to him, "Because I said, 'Lest I*

> die on account of her.' And Abimelech said, "What is this you have done to us? One of the people might soon have lain with your wife, and you would have brought guilt on us."
> – Genesis 26:7-10 NKJV

Jacob, his grandson, thereafter lied to his father, Isaac, deceiving him and collecting Esau's blessing.

> "Jacob said to his father, 'I am Esau, your firstborn; I have done just as you told me; please arise, sit and eat of my game, that your soul may bless me." – Genesis 27:19 NKJV

Joseph was sold to Egypt because his brothers lied to cover up his sudden disappearance. (Genesis 37:33)

However, each family was well equipped to stand united to overcome the enemy's attacks and challenges with faith in God.

> "Above all, lift up the [protective] shield of faith with which you can extinguish all the flaming arrows of the evil one." – Ephesians 6:16 AMP

The Spiritual Leader of the Family

God has called parents (the husband and wife) in every family to be spiritual leaders to their children. He expects the parents to properly guide their family in faith and the truth of God's word. This expectation is captured in scriptures like:

> "As for my family and me, we will serve the Lord." – Joshua 24:15b GNT

> "Train up a child in the way he should go, and when he is old, he will not depart from it." – Proverbs 22:6 NKJV

God expects parents to lead by example and guide children in God's ways. Be a parent who does what you teach, not merely commands the children to do what you have not yet demonstrated. Here are ways to become a spiritual leader for your family:

Engage in activities that boost your Christian faith. Spiritual activities like praying and studying scriptures together show your spiritual authority over your children and help them get acquainted with Christian life.

Be a good model of forgiveness and grace in the family relationship. This signifies to the children the importance of forgiveness in a believer. It shows them the beauty and the grace of Jesus Christ. A practical way is showing them unmerited kindness, creating a peaceful atmosphere, forgiving them for their wrongdoings, and teaching them to be of good behavior to their peers and elders. Before long, the children mature in their faith and understand and enjoy the grace of God.

> *"Be kind and helpful to one another, tender-hearted [compassionate, understanding], forgiving one another [readily and freely], just as God in Christ also forgave you."* - Ephesians 4:32 AMP

Build your children's faith by introducing them to the Bible early on.

> *"His parents went to Jerusalem every year at the Feast of the Passover. And when He was twelve years old, they went up to Jerusalem according to the custom of the feast."* - Luke 2:41-42 NKJV

Several ways to go about this are:

Expose them to Bible stories, making them interesting and relatable while highlighting the lessons. They will learn to adapt, understand better, and be eager to hear more. This way, you're gradually building their faith.

Playing Christian songs and audio or audio-visual messages constantly in their hearing helps build their faith and fill their subconscious with the things of God.

You can organize engaging activities, like Bible games, sword drills, quizzes, or puzzles. These activities make faith engaging and relatable.

The Place of Marriage

The family begins with marriage. Without marriage between a man and a woman, a family cannot be formed, and children cannot be raised. Marriage is God's holy institution and the basis of a strong and stable family built firmly on faith.

> *"Marriage is to be held in honor among all [that is, regarded as something of great value], and the marriage bed undefiled [by immorality or by any sexual sin]; for God will judge the sexually immoral and adulterous."* - Hebrews 13:4 AMP

> *"Then the Lord God said, "It is not good for man to be alone. I will make a helper who is just right for him."* - Genesis 2:18 NLT

"Two are better off than one, because together they can work more effectively... If one of them falls down, the other can help him up. But if someone is alone and falls, it's just too bad, because there is no one to help him." - Ecclesiastes 4:9-10 GNT

God's blessings are evident in every family that believes and has faith in Him. The gift of children is one of God's blessings given in marriage.

"Children are a gift from the Lord; they are a real blessing."
- Psalm 127:3 GNT

Parenting as a couple is a gift and something you should treasure and carry out effectively for your children's and the entire family's benefit. Learn to pray together as couples to seek God's grace and guidance in decision-making and resolving conflicts in the home. God must be the central theme of the home. You can achieve this by:

Bless your meals with prayer before eating. This shows that you truly appreciate God's provision and do not take it for granted.

Celebrate Christian, faith-based holidays like Christmas, Easter, Good Friday, Palm Sunday, and Pentecost Sunday. Celebrating these holidays as a family helps to build every family member's faith, especially the children.

Display scriptures in your homes as a daily reminder of God's presence. These scriptures can be displayed in pictures to bring the consciousness of God when looked upon. These reminders should be positioned strategically, like the bedroom, dining area, kitchen, and bathroom.

Notable Biblical Examples of Families Protected Through Faith

The Bible records families who experienced divine protection by exercising their faith in God. These include:

Noah's Family

Noah's family was saved from the flood that God had sent to destroy the world because of his faith in God. Genesis 7 narrates how Noah diligently listened to God. God instructed him on how to build the ark that would be home to him and his family, as well as the creatures God told him to put in the ark.

Noah's Ark.³⁶

"Then the Lord said to Noah, 'Come into the ark, you and all your household, because I have seen that you are righteous before Me in this generation." – Genesis 7:1 NKJV

Noah's family benefited immensely from his unwavering faith in God. Even when others mocked him, he stood firm, believing what God had told him about the impending flood and obeying His instructions.

"And Noah did according to all that the Lord commanded him." – Genesis 7:5 NKJV

He led his family right and protected them by his faith in God. God saw Noah's righteousness and faith in Him and was pleased. This shows that a family member's faith in God can redeem the entire family.

Job's Family

Job was a man who ensured his family walked in faith before God.

"When the days of their feasting were over, Job would send [for them] and consecrate them, rising early in the morning and offering burnt offerings according to the number of them all; for Job said, 'It may be that my sons have sinned and cursed God in their hearts." Job did this at all [such] times." – Job 1:5 AMP

Job never took any chances regarding his family, upholding their faith in God. The Bible records that he prayed and made sacrifices regularly on behalf of his children to ensure they were always in the right standing before God.

Joseph's Family

An angel appeared in a dream to Joseph, the carpenter. He gave Joseph instructions from God concerning his family. Joseph and his wife Mary, who had just given birth to Jesus, were saved from the hands of the wicked King Herod by their faith. The young family of three believed in God and protected from harm's way.

> *"Now when they had gone, an angel of the Lord appeared to Joseph in a dream and said, "Get up! Take the Child and His mother and flee to Egypt, and remain there until I tell you; for Herod intends to search for the Child to destroy Him ... So, Joseph got up and took the Child and His mother while it was still night, and left for Egypt." - Matthew 2:13-14 (AMP).*

Daily Family Prayer for Protection

You are expected to commit your family to God in prayers daily. Ask Him for guidance, protection, and unity in the family. Declare God's promises over every family member.

> *"The Lord bless you and keep you, the Lord make His face shine upon you, and be gracious to you; The Lord lift up His countenance upon you, and give you peace."* - Numbers 6:24-26 NKJV

Personalize these words into daily confessions for you and your family. The key is believing that they will manifest in your lives as you declare them.

The Boundaries Plan

The enemy attacks families through harmful influences affecting the family's peace, love, and unity. How can you use faith to shield against these harmful influences consciously?

Set clear boundaries that any family member shouldn't cross. For example, parents can set ground rules, like "No watching immoral or obscene programs, shows, or movies by any member, avoiding late nights, etc."

Discourage habits or activities that lead to spiritual compromise. Make a list of house rules that everyone must follow. These house rules should align with the Christian faith and create an atmosphere that encourages productivity and freedom in Christ. Good examples are family morning devotions at a specific time or a family gathering to listen to a preacher of God's word, with everyone getting involved and taking notes. These rules and orders should be kept as much as possible. If broken for no good reason, consequences should be attached (ensure that you administer and demonstrate love, grace, and mercy in consequence). Also, reward anyone who consistently keeps these rules, as it helps foster love and healthy competition while maintaining faith.

As Parents, there are ways to stop harmful external influences from getting to your children. Starting these at an early age will help your children get familiar with and accept your help.

Here are some ways to help:
- Constantly monitoring their social media involvement and vetting what they do on the internet.
- Encourage your children to actively participate more in Godly content or entertainment, online and offline.

The idea is not to come off as a difficult and overbearing parent. You must lead by example, prayerfully approach them, and let them know it's for their good.

Family Strengthening Meetings

The importance of the family coming together to strengthen their faith cannot be overemphasized. Occasionally, time should be set aside for the family to come together to discuss challenges and encourage everyone to discuss solutions from the Word of God while praying for one another. If a family member's faith is weak, overcoming the enemy's attacks may become more difficult. The aim is to keep everybody's faith alive and active so there is no opening to the Devil. The Devil knows the family is what makes up society and the world, so he will keep targeting loopholes to attack the family, desiring to weaken their faith and defeat them.

> *"Be sober [well balanced and self-disciplined], be alert and cautious at all times. That enemy of yours, the Devil, prowls around like a roaring lion [fiercely hungry], seeking someone to devour."* - 1 Peter 5:8 AMP

With this in mind, you and your family should critically look at potentially vulnerable areas where the enemy can launch spiritual attacks. For example, a lack of time for prayers and allowing negative influences like keeping bad company or following worldly trends in the family. Once you've identified these areas, take them to God in prayer, diligently work on the vulnerability, and set plans to make your family's faith in God solid again.

Faith in Action Challenge

The family, especially parents, can create a monthly faith-in-action family challenge where each member participates in a faith-building activity for that month. Examples of these activities include:

Performing random acts of kindness, like children doing the dishes for their siblings or parents buying random gift items for their children.

Memorizing a Bible verse together, especially after routine family devotions or returning from church services.

Write down and share personal testimonies of God's faithfulness with your family. This helps lift everyone's spirits and encourages them to continue in their faith.

Family Daily Checklist to Strengthen Faith

- I spent the stipulated time on social media today.
- I read a story about Jesus.
- I memorized or recited the weekly Bible verse.
- I said a prayer today.
- I am confident that Jesus loves me.

The shield of faith as an armor of God significantly impacts the family. It's one of the family's chief protectors against the enemy's attacks. A family deeply rooted in faith is strengthened against the enemy's spiritual attacks. However, parents shouldn't forget their role as spiritual leaders to their children, whom they are expected to protect and lead correctly.

Chapter 8: Testing the Source of Spiritual Influences

"Dear friends, do not believe every spirit, but test the spirits to see whether they are from God." - 1 John 4:1

The world is filled with various spiritual influences. People want to be a voice and authority on matters they do not understand. *"But these people blaspheme in matters they do not understand."* - 2 Peter 2:12a NIV. Today, the words and actions of many who pose as spiritual gurus don't align with the dictates of scriptures and actions, which has thrown many lives off God's preordained path for them.

Apostle John.[97]

How do you discern spiritual influences to ascertain if they are godly or worldly? What is the yardstick for measuring spiritual experiences to gauge if their sources and results are from the Holy Spirit?

From the opening text, John began with a warm greeting, *'dear friends,'* meaning this discussion is for no other category of people but the body of believers. Following John's greeting, the next thought is a call to discernment, which believers should uphold to guard against the dangers of negative spiritual influences. Knowing the increase in negative influences, especially those posing to be spiritually sound, John openly warns the church not to be ignorant and easily deceived. This is akin to Jesus' and Peter's warnings in the following verses:

"Watch out for false prophets. They come to you in sheep's clothing, but inwardly they are ferocious wolves." - Matthew 7:15

But there were also false prophets among the people, just as there will be false teachers among you. They will secretly introduce destructive heresies, even denying the sovereign Lord who bought them, bringing swift destruction on themselves. Many will follow their depraved conduct and will bring the way of truth into disrepute." - 2 Peter 2:1-2

What Are Spirits?

In 1 John 4:1, 'spirits' has to do with the source, effect, and result of every theology or ideology. This is why the Apostle John admonishes believers to "test the spirits." It's a call and recognition of discernment to combat the danger of spiritual influences. How do you discern the "spirits" of an ideology or theology in a world populated with many – some appearing harmless and godly but leading many to deception and spiritual harm?

First, it must align with the revelation of the scriptures and the character of God. Any doctrine, belief, or declaration against these two criteria is not from God. This is the beauty of discernment to the believer. With it, you can spot a fake from the real or a false from the truth a mile away. Discernment is not what you catch or wake up to. It must be consciously and intentionally developed.

Three ways to train your mind to discern are:

Like you would spend time with a loved one, friend, or colleague and begin understanding their thought patterns, discernment comes as you consciously spend time with the word of God. When you diligently study God's word, you become acquainted with His ways, mind, and processes. You can tell when an action, word, or perspective contradicts God because your foundation is girded on His truth.

> *"Let the word of Christ dwell in you richly, teaching and admonishing one another in all wisdom, singing psalms and hymns and spiritual songs, with thankfulness in your hearts to God."* - Colossians 3:16 ESV

Prayer is another pointer to help you develop discernment. In prayer, you can take up confusing ideology to God for clarity. This is why, as a Christian, you must build your prayer life because it's easier to pray to God and hear Him speak when you've exercised this mode of communication with Him, like with Habakkuk 2:1-2.

Relying on the Holy Spirit is the third pointer that helps you develop discernment. The Holy Spirit is your access to God. It means you're never without God, never without direction, and never without help. The Holy Spirit will always guide you from the flesh to spiritual activities, supplying you with guidance for discernment (John 16:13).

What Are Spiritual Influences?

Spiritual influences are forces or ideas that affect your thoughts, beliefs, and actions. These can come from God, the enemy, or human sources. Examples include teachings or doctrines, prophesies, signs, dreams, visions, the media, convictions, feelings, and guidance from spiritual leaders or individuals.

How You Can Be Led Astray

The Lord desires to lead you in the path of life, righteousness, and truth. However, the enemy seeks to destroy, distract, and deceive you (John 10:10).

> *"And Jesus answered them, "See that no one leads you astray. For many will come in my name, saying, 'I am the Christ,' and they will lead many astray"* - Matthew 24:4-5 ESV

> *"I am writing these things to warn you about those who want to lead you astray"* - 1 John 2:26 NLT

Judging from the above verses, some ways you can be led astray in this spiritually saturated world are:

Through Lies

Satan is a legend for bending the truth to fit a particular context. The Bible calls him the father of lies. For instance, he distorted the truth in the Garden of Eden when he asked Eve, *"Did God say, you shall not eat of any tree in the garden?"* Then followed with, *"You will not die."* However, you know how that encounter ended, and he still operates the same way today.

Through Disguise

In 2 Corinthians 11:13-15, Paul spoke about deceitful workmen, false apostles who mislead people as Apostles of Christ. They hide under the disguise of 'servants of righteousness' like their father, the Devil, who disguises himself as an angel of light. These individuals creep into the church as wolves in sheep's clothing (Matthew 7:15 ESV) by displaying their wit about the truth and then being given the right hand of fellowship by the church. Once they're in, they minister death and condemnation to the body. Apostle Paul calls their message *'demonic doctrines'* (1 Timothy 4:1), and their goal is to draw away disciples from the faith (Acts 20:30 ESV).

Through Sin

Satan brings temptations to cause you to err. However, he succeeded with Judas to betray Jesus (Luke 22:3-6). He failed when he tried the same with Jesus in the wilderness to derail Him from His God-ordained path (Matthew 4:1-11). So, Apostle Paul warns in 2 Corinthians 11:3 not to be deceived by the enemy's cunningness.

Through Signs and Wonders

If counterfeit miracles exist, there is an original, and the enemy is so good at copying the original that you can hardly tell the difference. The Bible describes his activity in these last days as – *"the coming of the lawless one is by the activity of Satan with all power and false signs and wonders."* – 2 Thessalonians 2:9. Since humans are desperate and their hearts are already failing, they're easily led astray by great shows of signs and wonders from false teachers.

> *"For False Christ and False prophets will arise and perform great signs and wonders, to lead astray, if possible, even the elect."* – Matthew 24:24

Through Stifling Faith

Every attack or persecution you face is an attack on the word you receive. The parable in Mark 4:1-9 revealed that when a believer undergoes an attack, it's the enemy attempting to steal it before it takes root and faith. The word of God is the basis of faith, and when a believer's faith is stifled, it's easier to be tossed by every wind of doctrine.

Discouragement from Reading the Bible

Know you're being led astray if anyone discourages you from studying the word using phrases like "You didn't go to theology school," "You are not educated enough," or "It's the Pastor's job to study the word." The Apostle John revealed a truth in 1 John 2:20, 27b ESV: "*You have been anointed by the Holy One, and you all have knowledge. But the anointing you have received from him abides in you, and that you have no need that anyone should teach you.*"

False teachers will always want to keep you in the dark by not letting you discover God or get to know His voice. They know that the minute you know God's truth, their hold on your life is broken.

Ungodly Teaching

> *"Now the Spirit expressly says that in later time some will depart from the faith by devoting themselves to deceitful spirits and teachings of demons"* - 1 Tim 4:1

Ungodly teaching will always produce an ungodly result. Unfortunately, it is the trend in some churches today. To blend with the world and to make the Church of Christ more lively and friendly, all manner of evil doctrines have been introduced to replace the truth of God's word. Now, churches desire to pull in a crowd by appealing to their flesh without a burden or concern for their spirits.

Today, some don't believe that they're forgiven and loved by God because false prophets have made them believe they have to merit God's love and mercy. Believers are subjected to traditions or doing penance to get God to love and bless them.

> *But when the goodness and loving kindness of God our Savior appeared, he saved us, not because of works done by us in righteousness, but according to his mercy, by the washing of regeneration and renewal of the Holy Spirit* - Titus 3:4-5

Individuals are led astray when they're taught the doctrine of doing things for God and not getting to know the person, Jesus.

Ways to Test Spiritual Influences

In 1 John 4:1, Apostle John admonishes that all spirits be tested to ensure you're not led astray. Furthermore, Jesus warned the church against false prophets as men that *"come to you in sheep's clothing, but inwardly they are ferocious wolves."* – Matthew 7:15

You can test spiritual influences by:

What Fruit Does the Spirit/Influence Produce?

Jesus, in Matthew 7:16a, revealed one way to test spiritual influences, *"by their fruits you will recognize them."* Apostle Paul in Galatians 5:19-23 gave a list of fruits or works that the flesh-centered life produces, followed by those produced by living from the spirit. The striking indication about the works of the flesh is that it's all for personal gain, and will always strive to use whatever means possible to meet that desire. Its works are the opposite of the edification and unity in the body of Christ. It is a far cry from Christ's identity and what He represents. In Matthew 20:26-27, Jesus showed His disciples that the pathway to greatness is not waiting to be served but willing to serve others. Only a Spirit-centered life will do that.

Is it possible for the false teachers to mask their fruit? Yes, but not for long. Eventually, they will revert to their original state, so watch out for the fruits of their lives, whether for or against the church.

Do They Align with the Scriptures?

This is another way to tell if the spirit at work in the theology and ideologies is from God or the enemy. Apostle Peter calls these false prophets' destructive heresies and warns the church strongly against them (2 Peter 2:1). Apostle Paul classified them as 'demonic doctrines' (1 Timothy 4:1). These doctrines are wrong no matter how subtly nice and pleasing they appear. They directly contradict the Scriptures and usurp Christ's authority. As Paul exhorts, *'For whatever does not proceed from faith is sin"* – Romans 14:23, anything that doesn't align with the dictates of the Scriptures or seek to glorify Jesus is not inspired by the Spirit of God.

So, listen attentively when people speak, not at their diction or how smoothly they appear in speech. Ensure what they say aligns with the word of God. For instance, the Bereans brethren *"They examined the Scriptures every day to see if what Paul said was true."* - Acts 17:11. The Lord Jesus is another example. The Devil spoke many good things to Jesus and even quoted scriptures to get Jesus to submit. However, His response wasn't just a counter to the enemy's temptation. It showed His understanding of the Scriptures and how He discerned that the Devil's words and intentions didn't align with God's word. (Matthew 4: 1-11)

To discern the source of spiritual influences, you must understand the Scriptures - their meaning and God's intention behind every word. However, knowing the Scripture goes beyond having a few favorite verses locked in. It's about knowing God, your identity in Him, and what He has accomplished for you.

This doesn't rule out getting exposed to a more profound truth of the Scriptures you already know. So, don't get offended when another reveals God's word to you in a broader light. It's not what Apostle John is warning the body of believers about. He pointed at those whose references, truth, and authority are not scripturally supported.

Does The Spiritual Influence Glorify God?

Everything in creation was designed to bring Glory to God. Jesus says:

> *"Let your light shine before others, so that they may see your good works and give glory to your Father who is in heaven."*
> - Matthew 5:16 ESV

> *"Keep your conduct among the Gentiles honorable, so that when they speak against you as evildoers, they may see your good deeds and glorify God on the day of visitation."* -
> 1 Peter 2:12 ESV

False prophets don't bring honor to God. However, they can present a false show of honor to move the hearts of men. If you watch closely, you'll detect they don't care about God's desires, only theirs. It's about "them," not the Lord's church. They always strive to promote themselves.

Does The Spiritual Influence Edify the Body of Christ?

"And he gave the apostles, the prophets, the evangelists, the shepherds, and teachers, to equip the saints for the work of ministry, for building up the body of Christ." - Ephesians 4:11-12

Apostle Paul revealed the mind of Christ to the church and why He gave this gift to the body for its edification. The aim is for the body to come to maturity and the fullness of Christ. Therefore, anyone called by God makes the building up of the body their goal. A false prophet doesn't have the flock at heart. He sees them as a means to an end and is uninterested in their edification. A church pastored by a False prophet could have a growing membership base but not a healthy one, as was the case with the church at Laodicea (Revelation 3:17).

Insight from the Holy Spirit

How often do you get nudged by the Holy Spirit? It's challenging for most believers because they have not yet developed their walk with the Holy Spirit to know when God speaks. In other words, their spiritual senses to see, hear, and act have not been exercised.

Do you want to develop your walk with Him? Know the word for yourself. The Holy Spirit would not cause you to do anything contrary to the word of God. Ask Him to speak to you, show you things, and be open to His leading because He will answer your request. Jesus said of the Holy Spirit, *"He will teach you all things and bring to your remembrance all that I have said to you. He will guide you into all the truth and will declare to you things that are to come."* - John 14:26b; 16:13 ESV

The Holy Spirit will cause your spirit to know if what you read, hear, or engage in is truly from God or another source. He will always nudge you to help you vet the many voices in the world. It's good to know that you have an inner guide who will never leave you because He is in you and will never guide you to error. Remember, the Holy Spirit will never lead you outside God's word.

Test the Spirit Through Prayer

> *"For everyone who asks receives, and the one who seeks finds, and to the one who knocks it will be opened."* - Matthew 7:8

> *"If any of you lacks wisdom, you should ask God, who gives generously to all without finding fault."* -James 1:5

Apostle Paul counseled the church to constantly pray without ceasing to keep their heart and mind on God. When you practice this, your heart becomes like an open channel where God can speak to you freely and guide you through His wisdom in discerning the things around you.

Godly Counsel

As Solomon declares in Ecclesiastes 1:9, *"There is nothing new under the sun."* Truly, you encounter no spirit that hasn't already been encountered. Before you, God has taken men through your path and brought them out to be light to as many who would walk that path. Now, it's your responsibility to seek these men out. Solomon counseled, *"Plans fail for lack of counsel, but with many advisers they succeed."* - Proverbs 15:22

Refuse anything that causes you to fear, be confused, hopeless, condemned, and ashamed.

Reflection

Discernment helps a believer gauge the source of every spiritual influence. It keeps you safe and ensures you're walking in truth and not a victim of deception in a spiritually saturated world. Test the source of every truth or evaluate every doctrine you hear through the steps discussed in this chapter. Whenever you encounter any doctrine through teaching, media content, or advice, test it against the following questions:

Does it align with Scripture?

Does it glorify Jesus?

Does it make my life fruitful and productive?

Does it bring peace and clarity?

You must be intentional with your processes going forward. Get a journal and record dreams, prophesies, or other spiritual influences you may experience, and run it through the questions mentioned above. This way, you can consciously test your life's and environment's spiritual influences.

Furthermore, you must learn to pray for discernment daily, asking the Holy Spirit to sharpen your ability to discern. Here is a prayer you can engage in daily:

Dear Father,

I need your wisdom, guidance, and protection in line with your word in 1 John 4:1, where you instructed that I test every spirit to know if they're from you or not.

Give me the discernment to know your spirit and truth in my encounters today. Grant me the wisdom to test the spirits of every prophecy, message, and teaching by your word, for it's the standard for evaluating all things.

Cause your Spirit to lead me in knowing what your will approves and doesn't. Help me discern false spirits that want to lead me away from you. Strengthen my heart to be steadfast in you continually.

Help me navigate this world of spiritual influence and to remain in your love.

In Jesus' name, Amen.

Chapter 9: Living Victoriously in Christ

"But thanks be to God, who gives us the victory through our Lord Jesus Christ" - 1 Corinthians 15:57 NKJV

You've been repeatedly shown how Jesus Christ freed you from the bondage of sin and law through His death on the cross and resurrection. He paid the price for all by defeating the enemy and his cohorts. By this, you are free to live victoriously as a child of God.

Jesus Christ.[28]

1 Corinthians 15:57 emphasizes how thankful and happy you should be to God for giving up His son, the Lord Jesus Christ, granting you the right to live victoriously. Most believers still live in the dark and do not know this great revelation God has given them victory through Jesus Christ. The enemy preys mostly on these believers who are oblivious to their victorious state in Christ.

Christ's finished work on the cross has empowered anyone who believes in Him to live victoriously. You have been given the right to live as an overcomer over any situation or attack the enemy throws at you.

Have you seen where a lion cub plays fearlessly in the forest when in its parent company? It's conscious of its parent's presence and power to guide and shield it from predators. Like the Cub, God has made each of His sons and daughters fearless and victorious in the enemy's attacks. However, don't get carried away; victory is not only about avoiding or winning spiritual battles but thriving in the abundant life Jesus promised.

"The thief does not come except to steal, and to kill, and to destroy. I have come that they may have life, and that they may have it more abundantly." – John 10:10 NKJV

You can see from this scripture that the purpose of Jesus' coming was for His children to have and enjoy life to the fullest. Take hold of this truth and envision a beautiful life for yourself and your family – God wants that for you. For believers in Christ, victorious living aims to walk in freedom by refusing to return to old patterns of bondage, standing firm, and constantly declaring their authority in Christ and exercising it in faith.

The Foundation of Victory

Christ's finished work on the cross set the foundation of victory, where sin and death were conquered once and for all. *"For sin will no longer be a master over you, since you are not under Law [as slaves], but under [unmerited] grace [as recipients of God's favor and mercy."* – Romans 6:14 NKJV. This foundation of victory comes from the following:

Christ's Death and Resurrection

Jesus' death, burial, and resurrection meant the law no longer binds you. This ushered in a new era of grace and mercy for all who sincerely believe in Him (Romans 6:14). The believer's victory and authority started on the cross because Jesus took on the sin of men when He died. He disarmed the powers of darkness entirely, which formed the basis of the enemy's attack on believers. Christ went to Hades to gain Victory and rose again to hand this victory over to believers.

> *"When He had disarmed the rulers and authorities [those supernatural forces of evil operating against us], He made a public example of them [exhibiting them as captives in His triumphal procession], having triumphed over them through the cross"* - Colossians 2:15 AMP

The Bible emphatically states that He publicly disgraced the powers that strive to constantly keep you in abject fear, bondage, and sin. So, you no longer need to fight hard for victory. Your fight and resistance to these attacks begin from a place of victory- the victory won by Christ for all who believe.

The New Identity in Christ

Your victory is confirmed in your identity in Christ. *"And raised us up together, and made us sit together in the heavenly places in Christ Jesus."* - Ephesians 2:6 NKJV. This verse reveals how far you are from the enemy's reach and his attacks. Jesus defeated him and his cohorts on the cross, and now, you are named with Christ as a Victor. Your identity has changed, and you should know that the enemy can no longer toy with you. See yourself as the son or daughter, untouchable, and now sits alongside Jesus wearing a victor's crown. Due to their changed identity, the enemy is no longer on the same wavelength as the believer. *"For you died [to this world], and your [new, real] life is hidden with Christ in God."* - Colossians 3:3 AMP

Christ is your new identity, and you must be bold and confident, declaring it to the enemy. Remember, he fears the word of God because it exposes his weakness, which makes it impossible for him to attack you successfully. The truth of God's word is part of the armor of God, the sword of the Spirit that destroys the enemy's attacks. *"For the word of God is living and active and full of power [making it operative, energizing, and effective]. It is sharper than any two-edged sword, penetrating as far as the division of the soul and spirit [the completeness of a person], and of both joints and marrow [the deepest parts of our nature], exposing and judging the very thoughts and intentions of the heart."* - Heb. 4:12 AMP

Steps to Living Victoriously

Christ has won the battle for every believer and made them victorious over the enemy. However, as a believer, you must know it doesn't end there. To keep living victoriously and maintaining your victory over the enemy, x-ray the following few steps:

Renewing Your Mind Daily

"And do not be conformed to this world, but be transformed by the renewing of your mind, that you may prove what is that good and acceptable and perfect will of God." - Romans 12:2 NKJV

The Bible emphasizes renewing your mind and consciously replacing negative thoughts with God's promises. This guards you from the enemy's numerous tricks and gimmicks to lure you from living victoriously. God's will for His children is continuously revealed throughout the Bible. It's left for you to constantly read, study, and engrave them into your heart to stay equipped to resist the enemy.

Speak Victory Over Your Life

This is not a one-time thing. You're expected to keep speaking God's truth over your life no matter the situation. Avoid saying negative words or accepting negative situations around you. *"Death and life are in the power of the tongue, and those who love it will eat its fruit."* - Proverbs 18:21 NKJV. The tongue refers to your mouth as a powerful tool to make positive declarations over your life. For example, in difficult situations, you can proclaim: *"I can do all things through Christ who strengthens me."* - Phil. 4:13 NKJV

God has endowed you with power as His child, so whatever comes out of you carries that power, even your words. Whatever you speak, negatively or positively, yields results. Activities like Bible reading, listening to sermons, praying, and watching faith-based shows or movies help drown out fear and fill your heart with faith, love, and power. When you abundantly have these in your heart, your mouth will speak them consciously or unconsciously (Luke 6:45, Proverbs 4:23).

Walk in Obedience to God

As a believer who wants to live victoriously, you must completely obey God and His word. It shows your faith in Him and the finished work of Christ. You shouldn't pick and choose when or what to obey, as obedience to God unlocks His blessings and keeps you protected spiritually. Read about the lives and testimonies of several great men in the Bible who walked in obedience to God. A notable example is Abraham, who was immensely blessed by simple obedience and faith in God.

Stay Connected to the Source

Abide in Christ through prayer, worship, and fellowship with other believers. As long as you stay connected to God, your identity in Christ remains firm, and the enemy fights an already lost battle (John 15:4). Remember, God never leaves His Children. The children have the free will to walk away from Him (disconnect) and reconnect whenever they realize their errors. However, you're advised to stay connected because the enemy aims to disconnect you and have his way in your life (1 Peter 5:8).

Resist the Enemy

Living victoriously means strongly resisting the Devil and standing firm against his spiritual attacks. *"Therefore, submit to God. Resist the Devil and he will flee from you."* - James 4:7 NKJV. You've discovered how to resist the enemy, using Ephesians 6:10-11 as the reference scripture. *"Finally, my brethren, be strong in the Lord and in the power of His might. Put on the whole armor of God, that you may be able to stand against the wiles of the Devil."* - Ephesians 6:10-11 NKJV

Live in Gratitude and Worship to God

Many Christians get carried away by the daily hustle and bustle of life and forget the goodness of God and His steadfast faithfulness. The enemy uses this as a loophole to attack and stop you from living victoriously. Gratitude and worship to God for your life reposition your focus from struggles and negativities to God's faithfulness and mercy over your life and family. This makes you constantly alert and aware of your victorious state in Christ. *"Rejoice always, pray without ceasing, in everything give thanks; for this is the will of God in Christ Jesus for you."* - 1 Thessalonians 5:16-18.

Living a life of victory brings glory to God the Father and bears good testimony to others. Faith, obedience, and a renewed mind are essential to living a victorious life in Christ.

Biblical Examples of Victoriously Living

The Bible is laced with examples of people who knew their identity in Christ and lived victoriously despite the enemy's attempts to derail them. A few examples are:

David

David was named a man after God's own heart because he ensured that he patterned his life in total obedience and trust in God. 1 Samuel 17 explains how he defeated the Philistine giant, Goliath, in a battle. *"Moreover, David said, The Lord, who delivered me from the paw of the lion and the paw of the bear, He will deliver me from the hand of this Philistine. And Saul said to David, Go, and the Lord be with you!"* - 1 Samuel 17:37 NKJV

"Then David said to the Philistine, you come to me with a sword, with a spear, and with a javelin. But I come to you in the name of the Lord of hosts, the God of the armies of Israel, whom you have defied... This day the Lord will deliver you into my hand, and I will strike you and take your head from you. And this day I will give the carcasses of the camp of the Philistines to the birds of the air and the wild beasts of the earth, that all the earth may know that there is a God in Israel... Then all this assembly shall know that the Lord does not save with sword and spear; for the battle is the Lord, and He will give you into our hands." - 1 Samuel 17:45-47 NKJV

David lived in total trust in God, which helped him to live victoriously. There was never anyone or situation that came against David and succeeded. Today, his life is still read and talked about by many. Learn lessons from David's life and challenge yourself to live trusting in God and the victory you have in Christ Jesus (David wasn't given the privilege of Christ's victory because Christ hadn't yet died on the Cross).

Paul and Silas in Prison

These men, recorded in the Bible as great Gospel missionaries of old, were imprisoned for preaching the Gospel. They never allowed their beatings, pain, and terrible situations to get the best of them. Instead, they praised and worshipped God inside the prison cells, and their faith led to their eventual freedom.

The baptism of St. Paul.[39]

"But at midnight Paul and Silas were praying and singing hymns to God, and the prisoners were listening to them... Suddenly there was a great earthquake, so that the foundations of the prison were shaken; and immediately all the doors were opened and everyone's chains were loose... And the keeper of the prison, awakening from sleep and seeing the prison doors open, supposing the prisoners had fled, drew his sword and was about to kill himself... But Paul called with a loud voice, saying, Do yourself no harm, for we are all here... Then he called for a light, ran in, and fell down trembling before Paul and Silas." - Acts 16:25-29 NIV

Abraham

Abraham was a man who walked faithfully with God. He obeyed God to an extent where God swore to bless him. *"I will bless those who bless you, and I will curse him who curses you, and in you all the families of the earth shall be blessed."* - Genesis 12:3 NKJV. Abraham exercised surmountable faith. His faith was attributed to him for righteousness in Romans 4:3. With this level of faith and obedience to God, Abraham lived a victorious and prosperous life. He enjoyed God's blessings, and the enemy couldn't come close to him.

Abraham as he's about to sacrifice Isaac.[80]

Shadrach, Meshach, and Abednego

These three young men were taken captives in Babylon (Daniel 3). They were highly trained and served in positions of authority with their friend, Daniel. However, King Nebuchadnezzar wanted them to compromise their faith by making them bow down to a foreign god.

Shadrach, Meshach, and Abednego.[81]

"Then a herald cried aloud: To you it is commanded, O peoples, nations, and languages,... that at the time you hear the sound of the horn, flute, harp, lyre, and psaltery, in symphony with all kinds of music, you shall fall down and worship the gold image that King Nebuchadnezzar has set up;... and whoever does not fall down and worship shall be cast immediately into the midst of a burning fiery furnace." - Daniel 3:4-6 NKJV

"Shadrach, Meshach, and Abednego answered and said to the king, O Nebuchadnezzar, we have no need to answer you in this matter... that is the case, our God whom we serve is able to deliver us from the burning fiery furnace, and He will deliver us from your hand, O king... But if not, let it be known to you, O king, that we do not serve your gods, nor will we worship the golden image which you have set up." - Daniel 3:16-18

These young men didn't give in to this attack (The King's command) but kept their faith in God, who came through for them.

Victory Journal

Now that you have learned what victorious living is, you can write down specific areas where you think you need to exercise this victory. For example, fear, health conditions, relationships, overcoming debts, and addictions, etc. Research suitable scriptures that address these issues, and daily declare them over your life. For fear, use this scripture: *"For God has not given us a spirit of fear, but of power and of love and of a sound mind."* - 2 Timothy 1:7

For health conditions, scriptures like Jeremiah 30:17 NKJV will help: *"For I will restore health to you and heal you of your wounds, says the Lord..."* Another scripture is Exodus 15:26b NKJV: *"I will put none of the diseases on you which I have brought on the Egyptians. For I am the Lord who heals you."*

Daily Victory Walks

As a believer who wants to live victoriously, start your day by putting on the whole armor of God. Recall chapter two of this book to refresh your mind on putting on the armor of God. Also, daily, say this victory prayer: *"Lord, I stand in the victory that you have already won for me. I trust in your power and promises. I declare that I am free, strong, and more than a conqueror in Christ, Amen."* Then, acknowledge and thank God for every progress you've made, no matter how small.

Reflection: A Life of Unwavering Perspectives

Revelations 21:4 clearly states Christ's promise to believers:

"And He will wipe away every tear from their eyes; and there will no longer be death; there will no longer be sorrow and anguish, or crying, or pain; for the [a] former order of things has passed away" - Rev. 21:4 (AMP)

When you read the Bible, several scriptures speak to the victorious life brought upon you by Christ. Meditate daily on these until your heart becomes full with them, and they proceed out of your mouth into your life. God doesn't joke with His words. The Bible says He honors them even over His name.

"I will worship toward Your holy temple, and praise Your name. For Your lovingkindness and Your truth; For You have magnified Your word above all Your name." - Psalm 138:2 NKJV

"So shall My word be that goes forth from My mouth; It shall not return to Me void, but it shall accomplish what I please, and it shall prosper in the thing for which I sent it." - Isaiah 55:11 NKJV

When you believe and walk in the finished work of Jesus, you can be sure to see the promise and fulfillment of a victorious life. These promises bring truth, life, and hope in challenges and are a weapon of attack against your adversary, the Devil, and his strongholds. Accepting the victory in Christ makes your battles already won. It's been done and dusted. All that is required is for you to live daily as a victor.

Do not let the Devil oppress you into thinking the fight is only beginning. The fight ended since the Cross, and you have overcome the Devil through Christ. *"These things I have spoken to you, that in Me you may have peace. In the world you will have tribulation; but be of good cheer, I have overcome the world."* - John 16:33

Conclusion

The Bible describes the enemy as a roaring lion looking for whom to devour. In other words, he doesn't go around devouring everyone. He seeks those who don't know about spiritual warfare, discernment, his mode of operations, or those who fail to live from the finished work of Christ on the cross.

It's not enough to read through this book and agree with the ideas. If you don't implement the practical and Biblical wisdom and strategies shared on recognizing the enemy's tactics, stand firm against darkness, discern the spirit behind spiritual influences, understand prayer and fasting principles, and learn to use the armor of God to protect yourself and others, then you won't see your desired results.

The principles shared in this book are not a one-off event. You must live by them daily as the enemy's attacks are constant. The enemy is always on the lookout for your most vulnerable moment to strike. Hence, this book is not a one-time read. You should return to this book as often as necessary when you need a refresher or to strengthen your perspective on spiritual warfare. The enemy is a defeated foe, and since he knows his time is limited, he will do everything to take down as many gullible individuals as possible.

The believer is never disadvantaged as Christ has already won the victory for them. The choice is yours to make. Would you rather live in this victory over spiritual attacks and their influences daily or continue to cower at the enemy's threats? Will you go beyond passively reading the principles in this book to actively and consciously doing them?

Since you've come this far, it's believed that you're ready to walk in the freedom and dominion path that Christ has paved for you. Let your life encourage others to do likewise!

May the Grace and peace of the Lord Jesus Christ be with you, Amen!

If you enjoyed this book, I'd greatly appreciate a review on Amazon because it helps me to create more books that people want. It would mean a lot to hear from you.

To leave a review:
1. Open your camera app.
2. Point your mobile device at the QR code.
3. The review page will appear in your web browser.

Thanks for your support!

Here's another book by Mari Silva that you might like

Your Free Gift
(only available for a limited time)

Thanks for getting this book! If you want to learn more about various spirituality topics, then join Mari Silva's community and get a free guided meditation MP3 for awakening your third eye. This guided meditation mp3 is designed to open and strengthen ones third eye so you can experience a higher state of consciousness. Simply visit the link below the image to get started.

https://spiritualityspot.com/meditation

Or, Scan the QR code!

References

Abundant Life. (2022, August 9). Understanding angels and spiritual warfare. Abundant Life. https://livingproof.co/understanding-angels-and-spiritual-warfare/

Bible Verses about Last Adam. (n.d.). Cgg.org. https://www.cgg.org/index.cfm/library/verses/id/3344/second-adam-verses.htm

Book of Ephesians. (n.d.). Bibleproject.com. https://bibleproject.com/guides/book-of-ephesians/

Miller-Haddix, B. (2007, April 23). What the bible says about positive affirmations – Confessions. Bible Resources; BibleResources.org | Christ Unlimited Ministries. https://bibleresources.org/positive-affirmations-confessions/

Thomas, D. W. H. (2023, August 1). The testing of Job. Tabletalk; Tabletalk Magazine | Ligonier Ministries. https://tabletalkmagazine.com/article/2023/08/the-testing-of-job/

turningpoint. (2022, February 8). 8 signs you're in a spiritual battle and how to win. David Jeremiah Blog. https://davidjeremiah.blog/8-signs-youre-in-a-spiritual-battle-and-how-to-win/

(N.d.-a). Discipleshipdevelopment.org. https://discipleshipdevelopment.org/wp-content/uploads/2016/08/lesson-11.pdf

(N.d.-b). Mattayars.com. https://mattayars.com/wp-content/uploads/2022/11/Lesson-3-Levels-of-Spiritual-Warfare.pdf

Arimoro, R. S. (2024a, October 21). The power of testimony. SAMUEL ARIMORO SERMONS, EXHORTATION, BIBLE STUDY, AND OTHER MESSAGES. https://samuelarimoro.wordpress.com/2024/10/21/the-power-of-testimony/

Arimoro, R. S. (2024b, October 21). The power of testimony. SAMUEL ARIMORO SERMONS, EXHORTATION, BIBLE STUDY, AND OTHER MESSAGES. https://samuelarimoro.wordpress.com/2024/10/21/the-power-of-testimony/

Gloriae, L., Sr. (2023, December 30). The power in the name of Jesus. Sisters of Life. https://sistersoflife.org/2023/12/30/the-power-in-the-name-of-jesus/

Image, D. (2020, March 2). Armor of god: What's the deal with the belt of truth? Destiny Image. https://www.destinyimage.com/blog/2020/03/02/armor-of-god-whats-the-deal-with-the-belt-of-truth

What is the helmet of salvation (Ephesians 6:17)? (2014, September 4). Gotquestions.org. https://www.gotquestions.org/helmet-of-salvation.html

What does it mean to worship god? (2020, June 1). C.S. Lewis Institute. https://www.cslewisinstitute.org/resources/what-does-it-mean-to-worship-god/

Cole, G. A. (2019, November 20). 10 things you should know about demons and Satan. Crossway. https://www.crossway.org/articles/10-things-you-should-know-about-demons/

Don't be ignorant of the Devil's devices. (n.d.). Revival.com. https://www.revival.com/a/176-don-t-be-ignorant-of-the-Devil-s-devices

27 Bible verses about God Freeing Captives. (n.d.). Knowing-jesus.com. https://bible.knowing-jesus.com/topics/God-Freeing-Captives

Did Jesus drink water when He was fasting for 40 days? (2015, June 16). NeverThirsty; Like the Master Ministries. https://www.neverthirsty.org/bible-qa/qa-archives/question/did-jesus-drink-water-when-he-was-fasting-for-40-days/

Riggleman, H. (2021, May 2). Fasting and prayer – an introduction and guide for Christians who want to pray and fast. Bible Study Tools; Salem Web Network. https://www.biblestudytools.com/bible-study/topical-studies/what-christians-need-to-know-about-fasting-and-prayer.html

Sanchez, L. (2020, January 11). What is fasting in the bible? How to fast & spiritual benefits. Bible Study Tools; Salem Web Network. https://www.biblestudytools.com/bible-study/topical-studies/what-exactly-is-fasting-all-about.html

Baker, L. L. (2022, October 19). What Does the Bible Say about Darkness? Bible Study Tools; Salem Web Network. https://www.biblestudytools.com/bible-study/topical-studies/what-bible-say-about-darkness.html

Baker, L. L. (2024, June 18). 10 Ways to Stand Firm in Your Faith and Defy Worldly Labels. Crosswalk.com; Crosswalk. https://www.crosswalk.com/slideshows/ways-to-stand-firm-in-your-faith-and-defy-worldly-labels.html

Ellis, M. J. (2017, August 17). HOW TO STAND VICTORIOUS IN THE MIDST OF SPIRITUAL WARFARE. This Redeemed Life. https://thisredeemedlife.org/how-to-stand-victorious-in-the-midst-of-spiritual-warfare/

Ufuoma Fijabi. (2023, May 7). How to Stand Firm in Difficult Times | Oneinspiredmum. Oneinspiredmum. https://oneinspiredmum.com/how-to-stand-firm-in-difficulty/#3_Ways_to_Stand_Firm_in_Faith_During_Difficulty

Wilson, Y. . (2017, February 13). How To Stand Firm Daily In Spiritual Battles. Kingdom Ambassadors Empowerment Network. https://empowermentmomentsblog.com/2017/02/12/how-to-stand-firm-daily-in-spiritual-battles/

Harris, B. (2022a, March 5). Adam Raised a Cain: Reflections for Parents in Pain – Brian Harris. Brian Harris. https://brianharrisauthor.com/adam-raised-a-cain-reflections-for-parents-in-pain/

michaelbensonajayi. (2021, May 19). FREEDOM FROM ANCESTRAL CURSES. Blogspot.com; Blogger. https://gracevinefamilydaily.blogspot.com/2021/05/freedom-from-ancestral-curses.html?

Miller-Haddix, B. (2007b, April 19). What the Bible Says About Breaking Curses – Bible Resources. Bible Resources. https://bibleresources.org/curses/

Blessing,. (2021, August 5). Blessing, Curse, and the Freedom to Choose | Hebrew College. Hebrew College. https://hebrewcollege.edu/blog/blessing-curse-and-the-freedom-to-choose-2/

Jake. (2015, July 7). 3 Types of Curses and How To Break Free. The Bottom Line, Ministries. https://www.tblfaithnews.com/faith-religion/3-types-of-curses

Schmidt, A. (2019, October 10). The Shield of Faith: Hope Mommies. https://hopemommies.org/the-shield-of-faith

Salsbery, S. (2021, October 7). The Armor of God: Pick Up Your Shield of Faith. Revive Our Hearts. https://www.reviveourhearts.com/blog/the-armor-of-god-pick-up-your-shield-of-faith/

akinnett. (2015, October 20). 4 Incredible Stories of Rescue in the Bible. Brentwood Baptist. https://brentwoodbaptist.com/4-incredible-stories-of-rescue-in-the-bible/

Mathis, D. (2019, March 19). The Story of Marriage in Seven Verses. Desiring God. https://www.desiringgod.org/articles/the-story-of-marriage-in-seven-verses

Chamberlain, T. (2020, October 22). What is Generational Sin? Kainos Project. https://kainosproject.com/2020/10/22/generational-sin/

Faith. (2022, November 24). Equipping Faith. Equipping Faith. https://www.equippingfaith.com/consider-the-text/develop-discernment

How. (2025, March 31). How to test spiritual experiences. Evangelical Focus. https://evangelicalfocus.com/fresh-breeze/528/how-to-test-spiritual-experiences

Kittle, L. (2021, August 4). 8 Ways to Tell If You're Being Led Astray. IBelieve.com; Salem Web Network. https://www.ibelieve.com/christian-living/ways-to-tell-if-youre-being-led-astray.html

Piper, J. (2016, October 4). Satan's Ten Strategies Against You. Desiring God. https://www.desiringgod.org/articles/satans-ten-strategies-against-you

Exum, J. J. (2023, February 18). 7 Keys To Victorious Living in Christ. Substack.com; Centered on Christ. https://centeredonchrist.substack.com/p/7-keys-to-victorious-living-in-christ

J.M. Troppello. (2021, October 13). How to Live a Victorious Life as a Christian - Mustard Seed Sentinel - Medium. Medium; Mustard Seed Sentinel. https://medium.com/mustard-seed-sentinel/how-to-live-a-victorious-life-as-a-christian

Obomanu, G. (2023, September 23). 5 Keys To Living a Life of Victory In Christ - Grace Obomanu Foundation. Grace Obomanu Foundation. https://graceobomanu.com/2023/09/23/victorious-christian-living/

Houghton, D. G. (1996, July). Biblical Foundation for Victorious Christian Living - Faith Pulpit. Faith Pulpit. https://faith.edu/faith-pulpit/posts/biblical-foundation-for-victorious-christian-living/

Ikhariale, M. (2023, September 9). How to Live a Victorious Life as a Christian - Michael Ikhariale - Medium. Medium. https://medium.com/@oziology476_69789/how-to-live-a-victorious-life-as-a-christian

Image Sources

1 Designed by Liuzishan on Freepik. https://www.freepik.com/free-photo/world-collapse-doomsday-scene-digital-painting_14541113.htm#fromView=search&page=1&position=1&uuid=86cfbaaa-2981-4bb1-9fd7-bcec43c324a3&query=spiritual+battle

2 Gustave Doré, CC BY-SA 4.0 <https://creativecommons.org/licenses/by-sa/4.0>, via Wikimedia Commons https://commons.wikimedia.org/wiki/File:Satanparadiselost.jpg

3 Photo by Tima Miroshnichenko: https://www.pexels.com/photo/a-grayscale-of-the-holy-bible-5199800/

4 Luca Giordano, CC0, via Wikimedia Commons https://commons.wikimedia.org/wiki/File:SAAM-XX105_1.jpg

5 Designed by Macrovector on Freepik. https://www.freepik.com/free-vector/massive-yellow-orange-explosion-bursting-into-blue-cloudy-sky-with-radiating-sun-rays_3815744.htm#fromView=search&page=1&position=0&uuid=e28e9c7c-5f27-442d-a736-3a6b4d8207a7&query=army+of+heaven

6 Denise Miller, Attribution-NonCommercial-NoDerivs 2.0 Generic, CC BY-NC-ND 2.0 <https://creativecommons.org/licenses/by-nc-nd/2.0/deed.en> https://www.flickr.com/photos/mercywatch/118098371

7 Metropolitan Museum of Art, CC0, via Wikimedia Commons https://commons.wikimedia.org/wiki/File:Breastplate_from_an_Armor_of_Francesco_Maria_II_della_Rovere_(1548%E2%80%931631),_Duke_of_Urbino_MET_sfeahCR(12-23-08)TR623-2-2008s1.jpg

8 shankar s, Attribution 2.0 Generic, CC BY 2.0 <https://creativecommons.org/licenses/by/2.0/deed.en>.https://www.flickr.com/photos/shankaronline/24498222789

9   Photo by Yaren Kılıç: https://www.pexels.com/photo/ancient-roman-shield-and-spears-in-istanbul-30564504/

10 Museum of Vojvodina, CC BY-SA 3.0 RS <https://creativecommons.org/licenses/by-sa/3.0/rs/deed.en>, via Wikimedia Commons https://commons.wikimedia.org/wiki/File:Late_Roman_Helmet_Berkasovo_1.jpg

11 Photo by Zain Abba: https://www.pexels.com/photo/gothic-sword-in-winter-19424928/

12 Jean-Jacques Feuchère, CC0, via Wikimedia Commons https://commons.wikimedia.org/wiki/File:Satan_-_Jean_Jacques_Feuch%C3%A8re_-_Mus%C3%A9e_du_Louvre_Sculptures_RF_4220.jpg

13 Andrewrabbott, CC BY-SA 4.0 <https://creativecommons.org/licenses/by-sa/4.0>, via Wikimedia Commons https://commons.wikimedia.org/wiki/File:Jesus,_Mary,_Martha_and_Lazarus,_St_Botolph_without_Aldersgate.jpg

14 Photo by cottonbro studio: https://www.pexels.com/photo/a-woman-praying-inside-the-church-6284758/

15 After Simeon Solomon, CC0, via Wikimedia Commons https://commons.wikimedia.org/wiki/File:Abraham_and_Isaac_(Dalziels%27_Bible_Gallery)_MET_DP835637.jpg

16 Glenn Marsch, Attribution-NonCommercial-NoDerivs 2.0 Generic, CC BY-NC-ND 2.0 <https://creativecommons.org/licenses/by-nc-nd/2.0/deed.en> https://www.flickr.com/photos/sphericalbull/5572969308

17 George E. Koronaios, CC BY-SA 4.0 <https://creativecommons.org/licenses/by-sa/4.0>, via Wikimedia Commons https://commons.wikimedia.org/wiki/File:Image_depicting_Apostle_Paul_on_July_1,_2022.jpg

18 Nicolas Régnier, CC BY-SA 4.0 <https://creativecommons.org/licenses/by-sa/4.0>, via Wikimedia Commons https://commons.wikimedia.org/wiki/File:Nicolas_R%C3%A9gnier_-_David_et_Goliath.jpg

19 A.N. Mironov, CC BY-SA 4.0 <https://creativecommons.org/licenses/by-sa/4.0>, via Wikimedia Commons https://commons.wikimedia.org/wiki/File:The_Apostle_Peter_in_prison.jpg

20 Lawrence OP, Attribution-NonCommercial 2.0 Generic, CC BY-NC 2.0 <https://creativecommons.org/licenses/by-nc/2.0/deed.en> https://www.flickr.com/photos/paullew/386607469

21 Designed by Freepik, https://www.freepik.com/free-photo/portrait-person-with-mental-disorders_11198922.htm#fromView=search&page=1&position=20&uuid=2a3d21fc-becb-4e20-8e87-816322673975&query=curse

22 Pier Francesco Mola, CC0, via Wikimedia Commons https://commons.wikimedia.org/wiki/File:Cain_Slaying_Abel_-_MET_DP-19625-001.jpg

23 Philip De Vere, CC BY-SA 3.0 <https://creativecommons.org/licenses/by-sa/3.0>, via Wikimedia Commons https://commons.wikimedia.org/wiki/File:The_Phillip_Medhurst_Picture_Torah_366._The_Israelites_leave_Egypt._Exodus_cap_12_v_51._Heuman.jpg

24 Photo by RDNE Stock project: https://www.pexels.com/photo/person-holding-silver-fork-and-bread-knife-5847688/

25 Александр Михальчук, CC BY-SA 4.0 <https://creativecommons.org/licenses/by-sa/4.0>, via Wikimedia Commons https://commons.wikimedia.org/wiki/File:The_Tower_of_Babel_Alexander_Mikhalchyk.jpg

26 Edward Hicks, American, 1780 - 1849 Jacquemart de Hesdin, CC0, via Wikimedia Commons https://commons.wikimedia.org/wiki/File:Noah%27s_Ark_by_Edward_Hicks,_1846_(Philadelphia_museum_of_art).jpg

27 COPTS, CC BY-SA 3.0 <https://creativecommons.org/licenses/by-sa/3.0>, via Wikimedia Commons https://commons.wikimedia.org/wiki/File:Apostle_John.jpg

28 Didgeman, CC0, via Wikimedia Commons https://commons.wikimedia.org/wiki/File:Christ-jesus.jpg

29 Lawrence OP, Attribution-NonCommercial-NoDerivs 2.0 Generic, CC BY-NC-ND 2.0 https://creativecommons.org/licenses/by-nc-nd/2.0/deed.en , https://www.flickr.com/photos/paullew/7203069100

30 Phillip Medhurst, CC BY-SA 3.0 <https://creativecommons.org/licenses/by-sa/3.0>, via Wikimedia Commons https://commons.wikimedia.org/wiki/File:The_Phillip_Medhurst_Picture_Torah_118._Abraham_sacrificing_Isaac._Genesis_cap_22_vv_9,_13._Goltzius.jpg

31 https://www.flickr.com/photos/internetarchivebookimages/14598336348

www.ingramcontent.com/pod-product-compliance
Lightning Source LLC
Chambersburg PA
CBHW051849160426
43209CB00006B/1218